*To Margot & Ia.
Best wishes
Caroline van de Pol*

HOW TO *Love* BEING A PARENT

Caroline van de Pol

Photography by Genevieve Edwards
Illustrations by Mark Knight

Edited by Vicki Hatton
Supplementary Illustrations by Chris Fisher

SATURN PUBLICATIONS

Dedication

To my wonderful husband Jon who made it possible
To my precious boys James and William who made it worthwhile
To my dear Mum and Dad for their 'unconditional love' sadly cut short

Copyright © Caroline van de Pol

This publication is copyright. Apart from fair dealing for the purpose of private study, research, criticism or review, as permitted under the
Copyright Act, no part may be reproduced without written permission from the publisher.

Although the author and the publisher have endeavored to ensure that the information is as accurate as possible, they accept no responsibility for any loss, injury or inconvenience sustained by any person using this book.

Published by Saturn Publications, 705 Plumpton Rd, Diggers Rest, 3427, Australia

First published 1992

National Library of Australia Cataloguing-in-Publication data:

van de Pol, Caroline, How to Love Being a Parent. Bibliography. ISBN 0 646 10938 3
1. Parenting. 2. Childrearing. 1. Title 649.1

Edited by Vicki Hatton. Typeset and designed by Mondo Graphics. Printed by Australian Print Group.

CONTENTS

FOREWORD   7
Professor Maurice Balson

SECTION ONE

1   **IT TAKES TWO TO TANGO**   9
Dancing with your baby
*Bonding — how important is it?
Learning 'the dance' and tuning in to your baby's cues
The benefits of 'wearing' your baby and 'touching' with baby massage*

2   **MILK, MARVELLOUS MILK**   15
Go with the flow!
*Breastfeeding is the ideal — but not for everyone
Unrestricted feeding — on demand and for as long as baby needs
Ways to cope with feeding problems*

3   **WHEN BABY CRIES ALL NIGHT**   21
Powerwalking in the hallway
*Newborns crying for help and how to respond
'Colic' — cures and coping
Relax mum! Some crying is 'normal'*

4   **THE FAMILY BED**   27
Make room for baby
*When baby won't sleep
Sleep deprivation — and what it means for parents
The value of the family bed and sharing sleep*

5   **LIFE CAN BE CRUEL**   35
But it is always precious
*Coping with the 'special needs' child (acute and chronic)
The extra parenting of a child with special needs
The effects of sickness or disability on the family and siblings*

6   **SHE'S JUST LIKE HER FATHER**   41
Moody, shy, brilliant!
*Babies are born with their very own personality
Types of temperament — fussy, easy, demanding
Effects of child temperament on parenting style and ability to cope*

SECTION TWO

1   **IT'S OK, IT'S JUST A STAGE**   47
She'll grow out of it
*Stages of development
Intellectual, social, physical and emotional growth in children
Delays in development and learning disabilities
What parents can do to tap into talents and special interests*

2 THERE'S A MONSTER IN THE HOUSE   **53**
And he's throwing a tantrum
Identifying types of behavior — temper tantrums, shyness and spoilt brats
The purpose of behavior and getting attention
Some strategies and skills — letting them know what you like

3 PLEASE DON'T SMACK YOUR KIDS   **61**
Bribe 'em!
The importance of discipline and setting limits
Teaching positive self-talk for good self-esteem
Techniques to try and rules to remember

4 MINE'S BIGGER THAN YOURS   **69**
But he started it!
Preparing the 'King of the Castle' for number two
Sibling rivalry in a competitive family
Teaching co-operation among children
Special problems of a one child or blended family

5 DEVELOPING A SIXTH SENSE   **75**
The art of mind-reading
Learning the techniques of 'active listening'
Messages we give our children are not only verbal
Talking it over — getting your children to express their feelings

SECTION THREE

1 WHEN GOD CREATED MOTHERS   **81**
He made them soft . . . and strong
Heartache of motherhood — to return to paid work or not
Signs of post natal depression or mother burnout
Strategies for time out and coping with 'having it all'

2 MY DAD'S A GREAT GUY   **87**
But he's always busy
Fathers play an essential role in their child's development
Changing roles of fathers
Effective fathering for busy dads
Single dads and stepdads

3 WHEN COUPLES BECOME PARENTS   **93**
Bridging the gap between work and family
Children as contraceptives
The changing face of families — blended, one-parent
Having fun as a family

A GUIDE TO SERVICES   **101**
Where to get help

SUGGESTED READING   **103**

ACKNOWLEDGEMENTS   **105**

FOREWORD

How to LOVE Being a Parent is a welcome addition to the important area of parent education. It is important because it brings to the field a comfortable combination of principles, practices and case studies which parents will find relevant to their children and which will increase their confidence in raising their children.

The author approaches her task from the point of view of a mother and a journalist. This combination results in a very readable set of articles, written with warmth and humor, and dealing with those important areas of child raising which all parents will experience in their children's early years.

I was particularly impressed with the range of views which were presented. Almost all individuals who have made a contribution in the area of parenting such as child psychologists, paediatricians and family therapists, are represented. Often their views are contradictory, inviting parents to select those ideas which they find useful.

A distinctive feature of *How to LOVE Being a Parent* is the way in which the author has successfully combined principle, practice and case studies. In each significant area, such as breastfeeding, a theoretical view is advanced and the implication for practice is suggested. Then, a parent who has had considerable experience in the particular area is consulted to validate the usefulness of the position advanced. Parents can readily identify with this approach and it greatly increases their confidence to also try the strategy.

The essential theme which the author communicates is that parenting can be fun, that children can be enjoyed and that parents can develop strategies and skills which will help them develop quality relationships with their children.

— **Professor Maurice Balson**
Monash University
August 22, 1992

CULTURE SHOCK...

From business lunches at the Hyatt to baby massage and finger painting on the farm.

When I opted out of the workforce and jumped into motherhood with the arrival of James five years ago, I found myself stumbling in the dark — sometimes coping, usually bluffing and often crying for help.

When my second son was born two years later, motherhood was a joy. I realised then that having babies didn't have to mean endless crying and constant worrying. With confidence, knowledge and reassurance, I learned new mums and dads could not only LOVE being parents but more importantly, confident parents could help create wonderful childhood memories for their children.

With the arrival of James came the invitation from an enlightened daily newspaper editor to write regular articles on parenting. I was amazed and encouraged by the response to my stories and was soon convinced of the need for an easy to read, entertaining and informative book that dealt with the many issues facing new parents.

While there are numerous babycare and child psychology books available today, they are often written by experts far removed from the everyday heartaches and joys of parenting.

How to LOVE Being a Parent sifts through all the expert theories, updates the best of the traditions and helps make parenting fun again.

In the book, parents will discover strategies and skills to develop their own styles suited to their life situations. The helpful tips will make their new responsibilities easier and more rewarding.

If baby's crying all night, toddler won't eat or Mum and Dad's sex life is going nowhere the book will tell you what the experts think, suggest simple techniques that work and relate actual experiences of real parents. Through the very frank case studies, the reader will find solutions to everyday problems such as the brainwashing motives of the children who won't let you sleep or the endless nagging to tidy up!

Everyone, from family and friends to people on buses and strangers in shops, is an expert when it comes to bringing up children. You will always find people, usually childless or past it, willing to give you advice on the best methods of discipline as well as ways to improve toilet training.

I remember an "expert" advising me to "let the baby cry, it helps him grow" and another telling me not to fuss over him so much when I was indulging in some interaction, "Just wrap him up and put him back to sleep," I was told.

Sometimes, however, the advice is useful. Take toilet training — the childcare bibles preach be positive, be calm, be supportive. I tried . . . then a friend suggested offering a treat every time the deed was done. Guess who was toilet trained in a week?

The numerous interviews with enthusiastic parents, the intense group sessions with new mums and the encouraging letters I received, suggested a book about babies, infants and preschoolers and their changing family shapes was needed by those facing parenthood in the 90s.

One recent Melbourne study of stress in mothers of children under the age of five found that 99 per cent were "stressed", most registering in the "extremely high" levels. Those mothers interviewed for the study suggested what they needed most was information about child development and behavior, skills to improve their parenting and confidence to carry them through.

How to LOVE Being a Parent is not about how to decorate the nursery, change nappies or sterilise bottles. It is about understanding your baby's unique personality, learning the art of active listening, really talking with your child and creating a happy home full of wonderful memories for your children to cherish and carry into their own parenthood.

The views of the experts, from paediatricians to child psychologists, parent educators and family therapists, encompass a wide range of philosophical approaches, sometimes conflicting or controversial but always challenging.

Above all, I hope the appeal of this book is in the pleasure of parenting, that it is not all heartache and guilt and that children should be cherished for what they are — not what you want them to be!

I never knew a baby or child could bring so much love. I had heard of the sleepless nights, the endless nappy changes and the timely milk depositing, but no-one told me of the overwhelming love I would feel, although my mum used to say that's why she had eight of us!

I love to watch my boys playing, peeping at them as they try on their dad's boots, teach each other to kick a ball or climb a tree. I love to hear their laughter, when they really get the giggles . . . I love to lie down next to them, to feel their soft skin and tiny hands against mine and to fall asleep together. I love the kisses they give so freely and generously.

Now, as my boys grow older, I love their enquiring minds, their innocence and their thirst for knowledge about everything from how God sees us from heaven to how to do a torpedo kick or duck dive.

How my life has changed. Another lifetime ago, my biggest worry was making the front page deadline. The days were filled with the exciting buzz of a newspaper office and interesting interviews. Now it's a matter of making "Willy Wagtails" on time and keeping fridges full and washing baskets empty. But being a parent does bring job satisfaction unlike anything I've ever experienced in my profession.

How to LOVE Being a Parent is primarily concerned with the formative years — from birth to five years — the most important years in your child's life. For the most part of the book I have referred to the baby or child as 'he' only to help differentiate from 'she' the mother. However, where appropriate, 'she' is used for baby or child. The book has sections covering the newborn and infant; the toddler and preschooler, and last but not least you — THE PARENTS! I hope you enjoy it.

IT TAKES TWO TO TANGO
Dancing with your baby!

- *Bonding — how important is it?*
- *Learning the dance and your baby's cues.*
- *The benefits of "wearing" your baby and "touching" with baby massage.*

SECTION ONE

1

Today my darling James is only two days old. I still can't believe this feeling I have, I am on a constant high, feeling so warm and so much love. He is lying in his basket right beside me and I can't stop looking at him. I have just fed him — about the sixth time and he is very contented. He is doing so well — feeding and sleeping and only crying for a feed or cuddle which I am happy to do all day long. Poor James had a bit of a rough start (what baby doesn't?) — the labor was long and complicated and in the end it was an emergency caesar. He is a bit skinny and I want to fatten him so it's good he is feeding well. This feeling of overwhelming love is unbelievable. I could hold and cuddle him all day long. I feel so privileged, so very lucky to be given this baby to care for — to do it my own way . . .

A S I look back on those words I wrote in hospital, I see that bonding was something that happened "naturally" for me and I think for James and my husband, Jon.

Some theorists suggest the first minutes and hours after birth are vital for bonding. We did not have those precious moments because of the difficult labor and caesarean, but we certainly made up for it. And yet I have heard other mothers who did hold and feed their babies at birth say that they felt nothing, and others still who were repulsed by the baby. While everyone is different, the ideal is being with and touching your baby as soon as possible, just as "rooming in" or keeping baby with you is now encouraged.

So, what is bonding? Perhaps another way to describe it could be "tuning in". I define it as that feeling of attachment that overcame me after the birth when all I wanted to do was hold and cuddle and comfort my new baby. As you get to know your baby and have more rewarding and responsive interchanges, as you "tune in", it is more likely that you will feel this "bonding".

But as mothers and fathers I interviewed for this book confirmed, sometimes the bonding or "tuning in" can take quite a while, even up to 12 months. All acknowledged, however, that it certainly made a difference when they did feel "bonded" with their baby.

After I got used to the idea of an elective caesar (knowing when and how my second baby would arrive) I did become excited and nervous. Most parents wonder how they could possibly love a second child as much as their first. According to my diary 20 months on, I was even "higher" after the arrival of William Jon. I wrote:

"Well, it is exactly 24 hours since our little baby William Jon was born. I spent all of those hours floating high on happiness and pethedine . . . all through the pregnancy you worry something is not right and then when you learn he is perfect it feels like a miracle . . . he does remind me of James. Already I have called him James. We have had a few cuddles and he slept in my arms this morning.

One baby next to us is literally screaming all the time. It's so loud it's distressing for me to hear, imagine the poor mum and the baby . . ."

GETTING TO KNOW BABY

THERE is much to be gained by learning about parent-child relationships and attempting to influence that relationship in the early stages, says Dr Jeannette Milgrom, Director of Clinical Psychology at the Austin Hospital.

"A developing relationship is like a river which builds up over time and breaks new ground," she says. "As the water flows it carves out new routes, following the slope of the land, and at many junctions the choice to go down one or another path is influenced by the smallest geographical feature. So it is in the developing relationship, that the smallest decision, which appears trivial at the time, leads to a flow that is hard to reverse. For instance, imagine a decision not to show your anger. Eventually this anger is so built-up that it explodes.

"Travelling on this river, many people believe that the only way out is to ride against the tide. That is hard work. The river is so fast, it often seems that nothing can be done. Sometimes it is possible, however, to intervene by steering properly and attempting another stream.

"More fruitful is to remember that small deviations have caused the problem in the first place. To have removed a little pebble, added a bit of earth at a strategic point early on would have meant that different types of interactions would have been created. So it is with the parent-child relationship."

In these early days of parenting, the baby must be our priority.

It should be like a courtship, a time to get to know each other.

Picking him up when he cries should be not only okay but a very natural thing to do. Crying is the baby's only way of getting his mother's attention. Letting him feed or suckle at the breast for as long as he needs is fine too, and taking the phone off the hook to indulge baby with a massage is a great idea!

Society confuses us with images of supermums with sleeping babies and sparkling homes and we confuse ourselves with the wrong priorities — polishing the floor instead of laying out on a mat and playing with baby.

I have heard of situations where the father has become angry that his wife seems so engrossed in the new baby and has little time for him, or he has felt inadequate in his ability to care for the baby. There are ways to overcome both problems; the mother must give her partner confidence with the baby — try not to interfere when your partner is in charge — and the father must be willing to learn and share the nurturing.

Dr Milgrom says both parents should try considering what the sources of frustrations might be in any parent-child interaction. The aim is to avoid an eventual tragic build-up of high emotions and perceived lack of alternative solutions, leading to overwhelming frustration.

LEARN THE CUES AND RESPOND

WHAT are the ingredients of a successful parent-child interaction from the first months of an infant's life? According to Dr Milgrom, it used to be said that the newborn infant was like a lump of clay, ready to be moulded by the world around it, just passively taking in what was being offered: "We now recognise that the infant plays an active role in social exchanges. He or she arrives equipped with a particular temperament and a whole host of skills including an ability to see, to discriminate between faces and voices," Dr Milgrom says.

"Responsiveness and orientation to the mother's face are easily observable in the first few hours of life. The alert newborn will imitate the facial expression of the first person he sees.

"Pictures of babies imitating pursed or widened lips showed the most wonderful interaction occuring. This beginning interaction is also seen in the first eight hours when the infant and mother can be seen looking and making sounds back and forth. From the first feed, the sensitive mother touches baby mainly during the pauses of sucking, so as to least interfere with the infant's preoccupation. By three days the infant anticipates a feed by reaching to the mother, turning his head and opening the mouth. By 10 days, crying can signal different types of distress. By three to four weeks, the infant smiles preferentially to mother's voice.

"From then on the interaction between mother and child becomes more elaborate as the infant shows more ability to appreciate the feelings of those who care for him, and organise and display his own feelings."

Dr Milgrom says a successful interaction between an infant and his mother or father, during the first 12 months, has been likened to a dance.

"Each partner takes turns, is 'tuned in' to the other and occasionally they move together," she says. "If we look at this interaction in great detail, this is the sort of pattern we see: A mother looks and smiles and coos at her three-month-old son. He is ready for some talking. He looks, then coos. His mother's voice becomes more animated, she moves her face more expressively. The baby becomes excited and moves all his limbs. His whole body smiles in excitement. The mother laughs. The infant tires and starts to look away, the mother decreases the intensity of her exchanges. She gives him a space in which to recover and waits for a signal that he is ready to start again.

"By six to nine months we see a more mature form of the interchange, with more balanced exchanges. Infants of nine months clearly show joy when their mothers show joy and sadness in response to sadness.

"In a successful interaction, both the mother and the infant attempt to get the other to respond to them. To quicken the steps in the dance, or slow them down in tune to their internal music, and to have their partner dance in a smooth ensemble. Of course, it is foolish to romanticise the

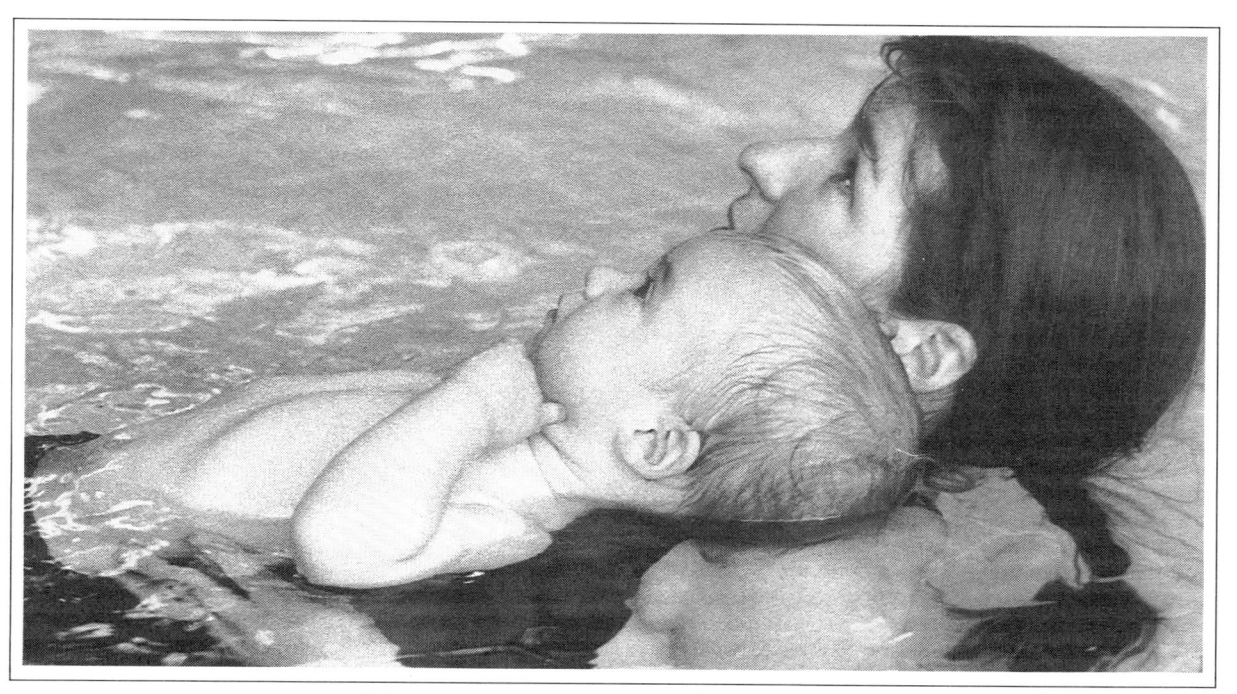

Babies love water and mothers enjoy the closeness.

parent-infant relationship and expect that it must always go smoothly. Being out of step sometimes can allow the child to try new things and feel more competent. Rather, the problem arises when the parents are continually out of step."

Dr Milgrom says it is the parent particularly who needs to be able to respond appropriately and immediately to the infant, as he develops this skill.

"In a successful interaction we also see a lot of parental stimulation (including physical affection), a lot of evidence that the interaction is gratifying to both partners," she says.

Parents should get down on the floor with baby and play, or at the very least look at them, touch them and interact. Remember, the floor is your growing baby's classroom.

Some parents say they don't feel comfortable playing with a baby or they don't know how to. It really is just a case of what comes naturally, rolling on the ground with them, tossing them in the air, playing finger games (peek a boo), lots of touch (round and round the garden, this little piggy . . .). Sound is important at this early stage — singing nursery rhymes, reading books or your favorite magazine out loud. A parent's voice is one of the most comforting sounds for a new baby.

PLAY IS IMPORTANT

A parent who is normally emotionally spontaneous and successful in interpersonal relationships will find it easier to respond to a child's initiative for social play, according to Dr Milgrom.

"A parent who gains gratification when a child reaches out and who gives her child's cues priority over environmental demands will find the dance comes more naturally.

"A balance between empathy and objectivity (seeing the infant as he is) is important so that the parent is not responding to a mythical child. And as the child begins to show more and more initiative in his preferences, the parent must be able to relinquish control and become less active."

Some things for parents to remember in establishing the bond are:

The dance steps can be learnt by parents, with the main one being how to observe your child. If the dance seems to be going wrong, however, it may be necessary to change the way a parent thinks about their child.

A newborn baby reawakens powerful memories in many people of earlier family relationships. This can sometimes form an obstacle to the developing relationship between parents and baby.

At times a mother needs to be remothered.

Giving birth often triggers memories of pleasant or unpleasant aspects of our childhood that we thought we'd forgotten.

All infants arrive with a certain emotional disposition so parents must recognise that different responses are necessary for different infants.

Maternal anxiety and depression disrupt the complicated dance. Studies show many depressed mothers gaze less at infants, touch them less and are less responsive. Mothers feeling depressed should be encouraged to seek help — from places such as maternal and child health centres, local council home help or perhaps a supportive and friendly shoulder.

Support for marital relationships at this life phase, together with exploring how to strengthen support networks,

CASE STUDY

A FEELING OF DEJU-VU

TAMMY had very different experiences of bonding with her daughters and believed bonding occured naturally with her first.

❛It was an overwhelming feeling of deja-vu and it felt lovely. I thought she was gorgeous. Immediately she became mine and she seemed to feel the same way about me; she was very fussy about who she would go to. Even now, although she is more outgoing, she still likes time alone with me.

My second daughter was born 10 weeks premature so there was little opportunity for immediate bonding and for me it took a long time to come.

There was such confusion over the birth and we had the worry of whether she would live or not. I didn't have this desire to hold her or have her close, I just wanted her to get well because she was so little.

I remember the kind nurses saying 'You can be here at 2 o'clock in the morning if you want to hold her when we change over the machines.' I said 'for whose benefit? If it's for me don't worry I'm okay, just let her grow'.

It meant that because of all that handling by strangers she was happy to be handled by anyone and it has meant our bonding has been delayed a bit.

I really suspect that bonding starts way back 40 weeks before the birth when you discover you're having a baby and you have all those lovely thoughts of your baby growing inside you.

It was almost 12 months before my daughter realised she could actually own somebody. She suddenly decided she would come to me rather than anybody else. Now she comes up and leans against me and wants her face patted or touched. It took her a long time to make her physical demands known. ❜

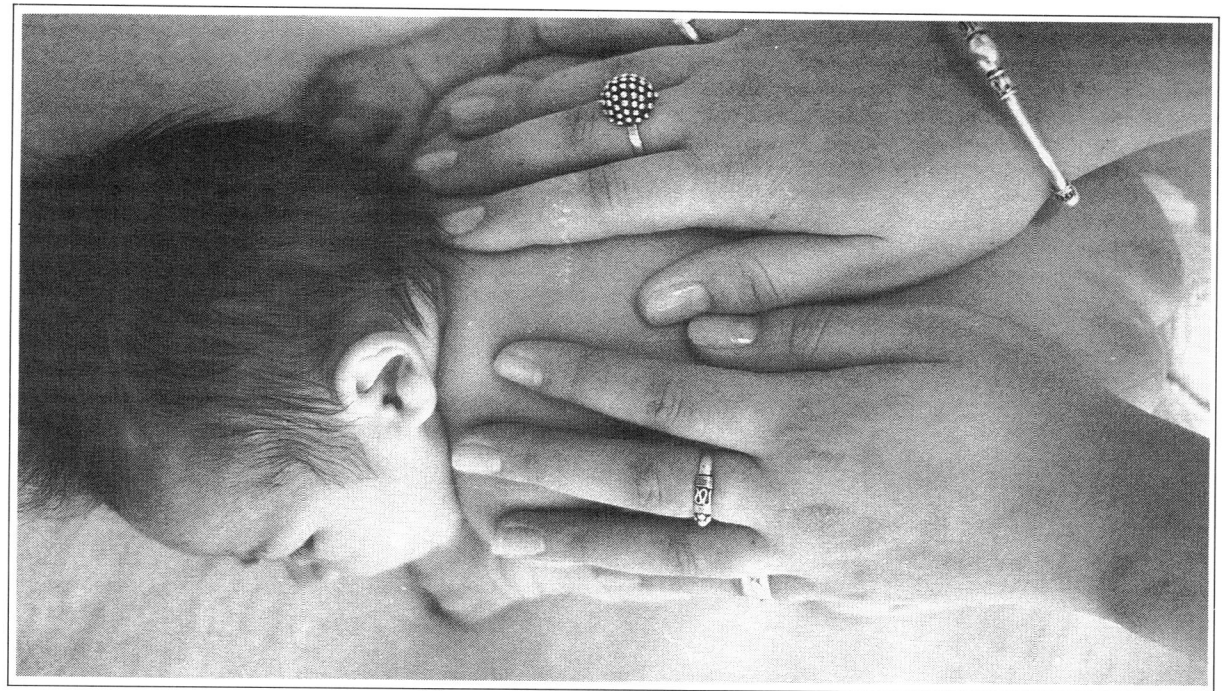

Massage is relaxing for baby and you.

will provide a stronger river-bed on which to foster the emerging stream.

WEARING YOUR BABY

CARRYING babies is part of attachment parenting and is important for bonding and development of the child, according to American author and paediatrician Dr William Sears.

"I believe carried babies thrive better," he says. "All babies grow, not all babies thrive. Thriving means growing to one's full potential, not only getting taller and wider but growing in behavioral competence. I don't believe there's any mysterious scientific reason why carried babies thrive better. If a baby wastes less energy crying he has more energy left over to thrive."

Carried babies are said to have a headstart on learning. A baby who's carried more cries less, and spends more time in the state of quiet alertness. This is the behavioral state in which a baby is most receptive to learning.

While there may be benefits of baby, some mothers and doctors do question the effects of carrying when it comes to carrying infants who are considered to be crying babies.

Dr Amanda Walker and colleagues at the Department of Paediatrics at the Monash Medical Centre found in a recent study that supplementary carrying of baby for at least two hours each day "did not appear to alter infant behavior over an eight week period, at least with respect to fussiness and crying".

What the 24-hour diary kept by parents of babies in the study, at one, two, four, six and eight weeks of age did show was "cyring and fussing behavior mostly occured between 4 and 8 pm each day with an additional peak between 8 am and noon (which disappeared by four weeks of age)".

HELPFUL HINT

The more you hold a baby, the more you want to hold him. Nature has designed mother and baby so that their needs are complementary. She, to cuddle and feed and nurture. He, to be cuddled and fed and nurtured.

MASSAGING YOUR BABY

THERE is growing evidence to suggest that baby massage facilitates infant development. Baby massage is not just a fad; it has been carried out in many cultures for centuries.

Babies have a good sense of touch from birth. Babies and young children need gentle, loving touching of their skin for reassurance and comfort. They can learn about themselves and their surroundings through touch. Parents can develop a closeness with their baby if they touch, rock, cud-

CASE STUDY
SLING IS SNUG LIKE THE WOMB

Jacky feels attached to her baby daughter, Anna, because she "carried" her even after she gave birth.

❛I carried her around with me during the day in a sling from the time we came home from hospital. She loved it and it felt good to me too. It meant I could do the things I had to do and still comfort her.

Anna didn't cry very much and I think it was because she was contented in the sling. It may have been the physical contact with me or it may have been the position she was inside the sling, which is not unlike the womb. She was definitely happier in the sling than in the cot or on the floor. They love movement and noise and there were always different things to see and hear as we walked around the house.

I carried Anna for a few hours each day for the first three months but after that she got a bit heavy and needed it less. I haven't another child so I can't compare it, but a friend who has a toddler and a newborn has borrowed mine and she says it's great. It allows her to have the baby close and a free hand for the toddler.❜

---

dle, caress and gently massage him. It will also often help baby to sleep better and relax, and it may ease constipation or colic. Gentle stroking and massage should be introduced very slowly.

Start by lying close to baby, let him feel your closeness and gradually and gently touch him. Massage only when you feel comfortable with it and hopefully the two of you will grow to love it.

Do not massage when you are tense or tired; baby will pick up these feelings. You want to put calmness onto the baby, so take the phone off the hook and plan to take your time. Anytime is a good time. Get yourself and baby into a comfortable position. Make sure baby is warm enough without clothes on. Use a comfortable chair or beanbag, a rug on the floor or your bed.

My boys loved massage and I always enjoyed doing it. We used to sit in a sunny spot after their baths, where I would massage them for ages.

One time I had William laying out on a rug after his bath and while I went to get the oil he dropped off to sleep. We let the massage go that time . . .

When you are feeding your baby massage his legs and back or gently touch his face and vary baby's clothing so you can touch his body.

Make sure your hands are warm and you may want to use an edible vegetable oil or powder on baby's skin. Use long, slow strokes one hand at a time. Start from the head, move down and across the body to the toes and hands. Get a rhythm going and talk to him about anything. Try singing softly.

FOLLOW YOUR INSTINCTS

• *Bonding usually begins immediately for parents and baby. If it doesn't, work at it with touch and play.*

• *Parents need to be receptive to baby's cues which start from the very first day.*

• *At certain stages the steps and skills of the dance will change; be flexible and let baby set the pace.*

• *As mother learns cues from her baby, he will read her messages.*

• *Baby massage is not only an ideal developmental tool but a great way of relaxing for both mother and/or father and baby.*

• *Wear your baby often if it makes him and you happy.*

SECTION ONE

2

MILK, MARVELLOUS MILK
Go with the flow!

- *Breastfeeding is the ideal — but not for everyone.*
- *Unrestricted feeding — on demand and for as long as baby needs.*
- *Is your milk in? Gaining confidence in your own supply.*

I wanted to breastfeed so badly, I looked forward to it with almost as much excitement as I did the birth. The experience was as special as I had imagined it to be, despite a few minor problems . . . nothing a heat lamp on a sore nipple couldn't fix!

A nursing aide brought James to me only a few hours after he was born and said he was ready for a feed. She was so kind and helpful, and very matter-of-fact. She had these big hands that almost covered the tiny baby as she helped him attach.

I cried as I watched him sucking, looking at his amazing face glowing with life. But then he slipped off — a common occurrence in those early days and the long-term result was the dreaded cracked nipples! What about that "let-down" reflux (when the milk is stimulated and comes down)? It can really stun you the first few times. For me though it was a good feeling knowing it was working!

James fed about every four or five hours in the hospital, sometimes more often when supply and demand were still being worked out. We coped well at home until we resumed a hectic lifestyle. As there were more and more interruptions to our harmony, James fed more frequently. (I did not make the same mistake with William and tried to do very little for the first couple of months while we got to know each other.)

I remember some days when James would feed every two hours. This was no longer fun — all I did was feed, change, lay him down for 20 minutes and start all over again.

The textbooks I consulted and the advice I received suggested it was a growth spurt and that it would probably settle down in a day or two. It usually did, but then it would start again soon after.

Growth spurts seemed to be coming days apart instead of weeks . . .

My second time round was easier and more fun. It was very much a case of "never look at the clock, let William lead the way". He was the boss and it was smooth sailing with a very contented mother and baby.

Looking back, I realise new mums in their maternity hospitals seem to carry on in a world of their own that has no place for outsiders or external events. The important things are whether "your milk is in", if you have an "oversupply of milk" or "how to increase your supply".

It was in this wonderfully supportive environment at the Royal Women's Hospital and Frances Perry House in Melbourne where I giggled my way through hand expressing and later "expressing with a pump". I soon discovered it was not only a means to the odd taste of freedom but also a way of coping with too much or too little milk.

While it is true breastfeeding for many mothers comes naturally and they go from their first feed to weaning with no problems at all, others may experience difficulties, ranging from engorgement to nipple soreness.

All new mums should remember that 99 per cent of the problems are minor and can be overcome with the right advice and support — either from midwives in the hospital or through your maternal and child health nurse. The Nursing Mothers Association of Australia also provides plenty of support to breastfeeding mothers and has breastfeeding counsellors who are available to talk to you about your needs. They also offer support through their new mothers' groups.

Hungry or not?

YOUR MILK IS JUST PERFECT FOR BABY

IT appears new mothers have got the message "Breast is Best" with about 90 per cent of babies being exclusively breastfed on discharge from hospital. But nearly half have been weaned by three months, with only 40 per cent still breastfeeding at six months of age and about 10 per cent at 12 months.

The Health Department of Victoria is very much behind the push for promotion of breastfeeding as are its counterparts in other states. It says breastfeeding should be considered a better way because:
• Human milk is the natural, safest and best food for your baby.
• It is warm and ready to drink without fuss and expense.

CASE STUDY

LET YOUR BABY LEAD THE WAY

FRANCES, a great supporter of the physical and emotional benefits of breastfeeding for as long as possible, says she often created a stir by breastfeeding her son until he was six years old.

'Unfortunately I did not have the luxury of being unnoticed, so it created a stir wherever I went and whenever I breastfed him in public.

Most women would breastfeed longer than the average six months if given support. But society makes our priorities cooking for our husbands, cleaning our house or having a career.

People even said I was a doormat because my child wanted to feed before going to bed every night. It would have been acceptable if I was tied to work in the same way of if I was out socialising.

Families, and even doctors, pressure women into weaning after six months. However, I was totally convinced by research I had done and growing up in the villages of Asia that children wean themselves when they are ready.

Every time my son was upset, whether he skinned his knee or fell from a tree, he would be soothed as soon as I put him on my breast.

I believe he is a much better child for having been breastfed for six years. He's far more adjusted and intelligent — in terms of his ability to interact with his environment rather than IQ. He's non-violent but confident with himself.

I suppose breastfeeding might not suit everyone and only women who want to should breastfeed but all women should be supported. After all, a baby is happier with a happy mother so it is her choice.'

- It contains many components that help your baby resist infection.
- The touch and closeness of breastfeeding helps to stimulate and strengthen the bond between you and your baby.

The Nursing Mothers Association of Australia provides many services for new mothers on a whole range of baby and childcare issues, but most specifically on breastfeeding matters. Many mothers have been helped by the association's newsletters, group meetings, individual counselling, phone counselling service and access to the latest literature.

BREAST IS BEST

BABIES have an instinct that encourages them to suck very easily in the first few hours. Ideally, your baby should be allowed to suck from the breast a few minutes after birth.

If problems with mother or baby mean that breastfeeding cannot start immediately, it is important to start as soon as the problems have been dealt with.

Very small or sick babies who cannot suck are fed by a tube. If your baby is one of these, don't get too discouraged. Your breast milk supply can be started by expressing your milk.

Most hospitals now practice rooming-in where you can have your baby with you all the time. In the first few days you should put your baby to the breast frequently. Short frequent sucking will stimulate your milk supply. Even though there may not be any milk for two or three days, baby will have enough fluid from colostrum (a thicker, yellower fluid which is more concentrated than mature milk).

Unrestricted feeding, where the frequency and timing of the feeds is determined by the baby, is now advised and it is also recommended there be no limitation of time at the breast.

Rigid clock watching is out and it is important to let baby feed as long as he needs because the fat content in breast milk changes during the feed. Initially the fat content is low, and the baby is getting a large volume of low kilojoule "foremilk". It rises towards the end (as determined by the baby) of the feed and this is known as the high kilojoule "hindmilk". The changing fat content is one reason for not interfering with the natural pattern of the baby's feed.

If your breasts or nipples feel sore you should tell your doctor, midwife, or maternal and child health nurse immediately — even if you think it is only a minor problem. Feeding in an incorrect position or problems attaching can cause your nipples to become sore or cracked. This can be helped or prevented by a good feeding technique — hold your baby close to you, body facing yours and his lower arm around your waist (baby's mouth should be directly opposite your nipple), mouth wide open almost all of the areola in the mouth. Some mothers may find a nipple shield useful, it is a personal choice.

If you have painful or lumpy breasts and feel feverish or unwell, it may be a sign of a blocked duct or breast infection. You should see your doctor about this. Early treatment usually allows you to continue breastfeeding.

After the demand and supply mechanisms of your breastmilk settles down your milk may start to look thin and blue. This is how breast milk looks normally. Within five or six weeks most babies settle into a fairly regular pattern and your milk supply adjusts to demand. It is best to nurse your baby when he is hungry. This is sometimes called "demand feeding", or feeding according to need. Don't worry if you seem to have too much milk or if it flows too rapidly or slowly at first. You and your baby will adjust to each other gradually.

Another important consideration is the new view on the necessity of "burping" your baby after a feed. Mothers sometimes spend a long time over a feed trying to get the baby's wind up. If the baby is feeding contentedly there is no need to do anything about wind. Another baby, however, may want a short rest between breasts and may or may not bring up wind. In many countries in the world wind is not recognised as a problem and nothing is done about "burping".

Some babies will need fewer feeds at night after a few weeks, but others will still need several night feeds for some time. If you are awakened at night, try to get extra rest during the day. As your baby grows, you may notice spurts in growth and/or appetite when he seems hungry and may gain weight more rapidly for a week or so. At other times weight gain may be slow. If you feed according to need your breast milk supply will adjust naturally. Mothers often worry unnecessarily about whether their baby is having enough milk. Weight gain can be irregular. If your baby looks satisfied and sleeps soundly after most feeds, has six to nine wet nappies a day, if he doesn't seem to cry for food a lot or suck his fists hungrily he is probably having enough.

If you think your baby is hungry, take a day or so to rest more and offer him the breast more frequently. You could try small "top up" feeds at the breast if he wakes less than an hour after a feed. Ask the advice of your health nurse or the NMAA before giving your baby any formula by bottle.

As well as plenty of rest, the new mother needs regular, nutritious meals and should drink plenty of water.

As easy as it may sound, do try to keep housework to a minimum and meal preparation as simple as possible.

Usually breastmilk is all your baby needs for the first four to six months. In very hot weather, though you could also offer him cool boiled water by bottle or spoon. Again, your maternal and child health nurse can provide you with the appropriate advice for starting solids.

For those women returning to work, breastfeeding can be continued if you wish. If appropriate, mother should breastfeed immediately before and after work and leave some expressed breast milk in a bottle for the time that you are away.

When you stop breastfeeding is for you and your child to decide and again you might seek advice from the experts. However, once weaning has been introduced either by increasing more solid food at the appropriate age or drinks from a bottle or a cup your breast milk will gradually decrease. It is possible, however, to continue one or two feeds a day for as long as you wish. It is widely agreed that the best way of weaning is slowly and naturally — you will not have painful breasts and your baby will accept the change more easily.

BREAST OR BOTTLE? GO WITH WHAT FEELS RIGHT

THERE are many good books available that deal solely with breastfeeding. Here is some information for new mothers to consider.

Human breastmilk is tailor-made for baby; it contains just the right amount of protein, carbohydrates, minerals and vitamins to sustain your growing baby. But quite apart from its nutritional worth, breastfeeding makes sense for these reasons:

• Breast-fed babies are less prone to illness than bottle-fed babies.

• Colostrum and mother's milk contain antibodies that in the first few days of life provide protection against infection.

• Breastmilk is more quickly and easily digested than cow's milk.

• Breastfeeding is good for your figure and evidence suggests it can protect against cancer.

Sometimes, even with the best care in the world, a mother may experience problems with breastfeeding or breast or nipple soreness. Here are some suggestions for dealing with those problems:

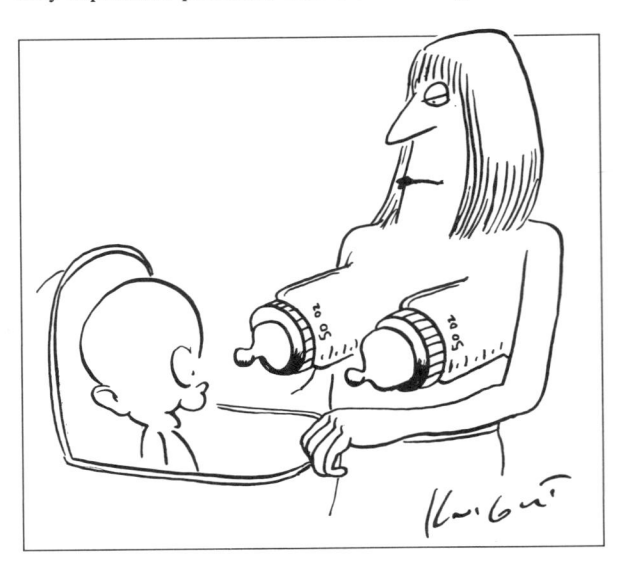

REFUSING THE BREAST — one of the most common reasons is that the baby has difficulty breathing. Make sure your breast is not covering his nose or he may be fretful. Calm him down first.

SUCKY BABIES — for many babies sucking on their mother's breast is the most pleasant experience of the day. You'll soon learn to distinguish between sucking for food and sucking for comfort.

SLEEPING THROUGH FEEDS — if your baby is not

interested in feeding, still try suckling your baby for about five minutes at each breast at each feed. If the baby goes to sleep, don't worry; it is a good sign he is contented and doing well.

SORE NIPPLES — try to always make sure that the baby has the nipple and areola well into his mouth. Letting the baby come off naturally will help prevent nipple soreness but if you have to take the baby off, do it gently by inserting your little finger in the side of his mouth, pull it away and hold it there. If you try to keep your nipples as dry as possible between feeds, you will minimise the possibility of any problems. A good technique to remember here is to express a little milk and rub onto each nipple before and after feeding. Oils and creams may be useful for some mothers.

INCREASING SUPPLY — you can help promote a good supply by resting as much as possible, particularly during the first weeks. This really is a situation where you should sit rather than stand, lie rather than sit.

HELPFUL HINT

Many dentists are seeing the effects of babies and toddlers who are given bottles of milk, cordial or juice to suck on constantly, whether it's to help get them to sleep at night or keep them quiet in prams at the shopping centre.

The sugar content in the drinks and residue on the teats causes decay in young teeth.

A bottle or cup with teat should only be given when drinking and when the drink is finished taken from the baby or child.

CASE STUDY

FEEDING IN THE CAR PARK

BARBARA is somewhat of an expert when it comes to breastfeeding, having had six children spread over 20 years.

*‛I tried breastfeeding with my first child but was not very successful. In hindsight, the advice I received in hospital back then was pretty shocking. The baby was brought to you every four hours, fed and test-weighed and if the nurse thought it wasn't enough the baby was given a bottle. The hospital was not quite at the forefront of obstetrics although I think it was common practice back then.

It didn't do a good deal for morale but then I wasn't particularly concerned because I didn't know too much and most of the other mothers weren't doing too well either.

After the birth of my second child I was in for another shock, but one of a different kind. I kept waiting for the nurses to change her nappy or bath her and then they said 'no, you do it'. It was strange but it was wonderful and I left hospital with so much confidence.

As far as breastfeeding the second time round, all I thought was 'I would if I could'. Having failed once I was not going to face failure again in a hurry but I went on to feed successfully for 12 months until I weaned so we could have another child.

Our third baby was 'the textbook baby'. She made you feel that babies were wonderful. I noticed how 'good' she was because my second child had been colicky. I suppose I worried over her because she was so small and because of the fertility treatment I had had and I worried that she was okay.

Breastfeeding just has to be the best thing to do in all ways — it's good for the baby, it's good for the mother and I think it's good for siblings. It's so convenient. It frees you up to sit with a toddler or older child while you feed and you can talk and play with them while feeding. You can go anywhere with just a nappy and a bag. You are freer to do the things you need to do with a toddler like getting outside, visiting or walking to the park.

I think the older children accepted a new baby because they had always been around babies and seen a lot of breastfeeding at the Nursing Mothers meetings I attended. I think smaller families accentuate the problems of sibling rivalry.

As far as getting the six of them organised and ready, I think breastfeeding speeds up the process. You can always finish the feed in the car park at kinder! The only thing I couldn't do while breastfeeding was plait the girls' hair. I could make sandwiches, get breakfast or whatever — the wonderful Meh Tai (a baby sling) helped.

I fed my fourth child up until number five was born. I was too tired to wean and I had been reassured that breastfeeding through pregnancy was fine. When the baby and I came home the day after the birth my older child snuggled next to me for a feed but I explained the new baby would now be breastfed and suggested to her 'wouldn't you rather have a sweet?' and with that she was weaned . . .‚*

Giving them "real" food (messy but fun).

For whatever reasons, some women and parents will choose to bottlefeed their babies at some stage in their lives. There are some women who have no desire to breastfeed or if they do try, feel they cannot continue.

Motherhood is hard enough without women worrying themselves silly over breast or bottle and the best time to wean.

Weaning from breast or bottle is easy when you and your baby are ready. Age has little to do with it!

I know one mother who says she always felt she was judged harshly because she chose to bottlefeed her new baby.

This very caring and loving, but bottlefeeding, mother who got sick and tired of people asking why she wasn't breastfeeding soon kept them quiet with the shocking news that she had no nipples!

Women who do bottlefeed their babies claim they still enjoy a wonderful and strong "attachment" and bonding that is said to only come from breastfeeding. As one mother puts it "we love our babies just as much as anyone else . . . breastfeeding should be an option and not the only way . . ." Non-breastfeeders say it has very good advantages, not the least being the involvement of the father who can take his turn at feeding and nursing the baby.

Bottle-feeding, however, can be hard work and the trick to it all is being organised — buying up lots of supplies from bottles to sterilising equipment and cleaning brushes.

A few tips to make it easier for the bottlefeeding mum:

- Buy at least six bottles, and a good supply of teats.

- Always mix formula according to instructions and stock up on formula and perhaps look at buying wholesale.

- Beware heating bottles and always check for correct temperature.
- Follow sterilising instructions closely.

LET NATURE LEAD THE WAY

- *Most mothers worry that they do not have enough milk — develop confidence in your milk and your supply.*

- *When breastfeeding make sure your diet is balanced and rich in protein — drink plenty of fluids, especially water.*

- *Try expressing your milk and storing for emergencies — or a night out.*

- *Leave the housework and lie down.*

- *Go with the flow — bottle or breast is mother's choice.*

- *Keep spare bottles, teats and the works for emergencies — be prepared to lose them out of prams, under cots and obscure places.*

- *Wean when you and baby are ready.*

- *Don't be afraid to seek help from people like your maternal and child health nurse or the Nursing Mothers' Association of Australia.*

SECTION ONE

3

WHEN BABY CRIES ALL NIGHT
Powerwalking in the hallway

- *Newborns crying for help and how to respond.*
- *'Colic' — cures and coping.*
- *Relax mum! Some crying is 'normal'.*

EVERY mother probably knows that terrible ache when their baby cries and that inexhaustible search for a magical cure for a baby who cries a lot.

I certainly put many of the suggested remedies to the test — from wrapping tightly to rocking; deep bath relaxation to baby massage. Some worked some of the time, but not all of them worked all of the time! Like many parents I felt if only I could do the right thing, the crying would stop.

Parents need to recognise, however, that the baby's crying is the only way they can attract attention. Hence, it has been described as an "acoustic umbilical cord" between the helpless baby and carer. Crying, like babbling, is the baby's language and way of communicating and for this reason I believe a new baby should not be left to cry. As the baby grows, the mother will learn to recognise what his particular cry means.

While I believe it's not good to leave baby to cry, it is also important that parents do not become over-anxious, or punish themselves about what is considered "normal" crying.

One school of thought is that all newborn babies will cry — some more than others — and that two to three hours of crying a day is in fact the "norm". If there is significantly more crying the parents will also need to find their own strategies for coping and responding.

I know that with me, one little cry and I'm up to check on the baby — all fears and doubts flooding into my mind. But even when the baby has settled, like most I often wondered 'is he all right', as Sudden Infant Death Syndrome (SIDS) or Cot Death is a very real fear. Who could ever forget that first night at home with a new baby? How many times did I check he was okay and just give a little poke to check he was still breathing?

And those first few weeks when all I seemed to be doing was powerwalking with a crying baby — up and down the hallway at 3 am. I still smile as I remember this dance we did together to our favorite classical music or the more upbeat rap number. The boys loved music and even the SBS test pattern music came in handy sometimes. However, the old musical mobile above the cot was never quite up to scratch.

Looking back, I remember being worn out and tired by constant crying (both his and mine). My "first and fussy" baby seemed to cry a lot and then I would join him in tears. All the bottom-patting, rocking and singing I could muster would not do any good. The thing I found for my sanity was to walk away, take a deep breath and count to 50. Or, if that didn't work I'd do some sit-ups or weed the garden and try again later.

I remember one morning at 5 am sitting, nursing, rocking and crying — saying "I can't handle it any more". There were visitors coming for the day and, in hindsight, the tears and unsettled baby were really the result of my anxiety over whether the house would be sparkling enough and whether my baby would be sleeping peacefully while everyone admired him and I served afternoon tea. How ridiculous it

Accept the crying so you will enjoy the quiet times.

all seems now! New mothers don't need that kind of pressure and they don't need the well-meaning advice such as "don't pick him up every time he cries, you'll spoil him" and "you're making a rod for your own back".

On yet another occasion my husband came home from work to find both James and I lying on the bed, crying.

> **I was so tired and felt like a failure. Why couldn't I stop my baby from crying?**

It was like a vicious circle; the baby sensed the anxiety and became more unsettled, and the constant crying caused more anxiety in me.

Jon took him for a drive (a habit we did not get into but resorted to once or twice) and all I did was worry that they would have an accident.

One piece of advice I received which I particularly liked and which goes some way to understanding whether the child's crying is "normal" or not, was to keep a cry chart.

On a special chart, record your baby's crying: what time, how long, what efforts were made to settle the baby and the results. It was not unlike a sleep clock I kept of James' first weeks which helped me realise he was sleeping more than I thought. So it is with the crying chart.

While parents often say their baby cries all the time, the chart shows that in many cases the total crying does not amount to more than two hours a day.

Another important observation has been that the more frantic manouevres a mother uses to try to quiet the baby, the more it cries. Also, if the parents allow for a certain amount of crying and intersperse their own quiet, calm attempts to soothe the infant periodically, the crying often settles down to the acceptable two hours a day. This period of crying then starts to decrease over time and by 10 weeks is just about gone.

CASE STUDY

A NIGHTMARE FOR NEW PARENTS

FOR Jenny, and her husband, the first six months of parenthood were a nightmare. Instead of the happy smiling baby they had imagined, their daughter cried and screamed for hours.

'She's my first, and maybe only, and I wouldn't say I was a paranoid first mother because initially I was relaxed and confident.

She basically screamed for six months. She would cry for 20 hours a day and she didn't sleep. From what I knew and from what I was told she had colic. I tried everything I could think of, I tried doctors, specialists and naturopaths; I changed diets, I tried massage, every patent potion you could find. I remember thinking 'three months and it will all be over'. She went to seven months. Whether you held her or not she screamed.

I went to see four doctors and specialists. One said to me 'all babies cry' and pushed me out the door with no help or advice.

My baby seemed to be in agony whether you held her or left her. The thing that hurt also was the undermining relatives saying 'she's got you on a string' and yet I heard other mothers say they wouldn't leave their baby to cry.

People will say 'oh, it's you', but I stayed pretty calm and coped for three months and I was still quite happy and just accepted it. But when it got to six months . . . I can remember very early one morning thinking 'well, a sharp knife and it's all over for me, no mess and nothing to explain'. I never thought of hurting my baby but I was suicidal.

Breastfeeding was the only thing I would not stop doing, although I altered my diet and cut out dairy products. She thrived on my milk. Dealing with the professionals was very frustrating. I remember thinking 'you're hearing me but you're not really listening'. I was not looking for sympathy and I was not an hysterical mother. I was just looking for support but it wasn't there.

I finally went to a paediatrician and I just wept and wept. He said leave her to scream, and I said 'we do'. He said: — 'no leave her 24 to 36 hours . . .' I said I couldn't and he suggested sedation which we finally took on.

During that time I lost quite a few kilos and I was a wreck. It was a nightmare. I don't think anybody really understood except one close girlfriend who would encourage me and say 'you're doing a good job'.

I had a break on Saturday mornings, I didn't sleep but I would still go to work because it was my only outlet. Relatives would offer help but they could do less for her. The breastfeeding was what settled her and my husband was always saying 'shove it in her mouth'. You have other people saying 'this worked for me' and it makes you feel like a failure.

The most upsetting thing was there was such little understanding from the professional people and they brushed it off. I have heard of some babies crying like mine but I think most people don't admit to their babies being like that or they block it out because they see themselves as being a failure.'

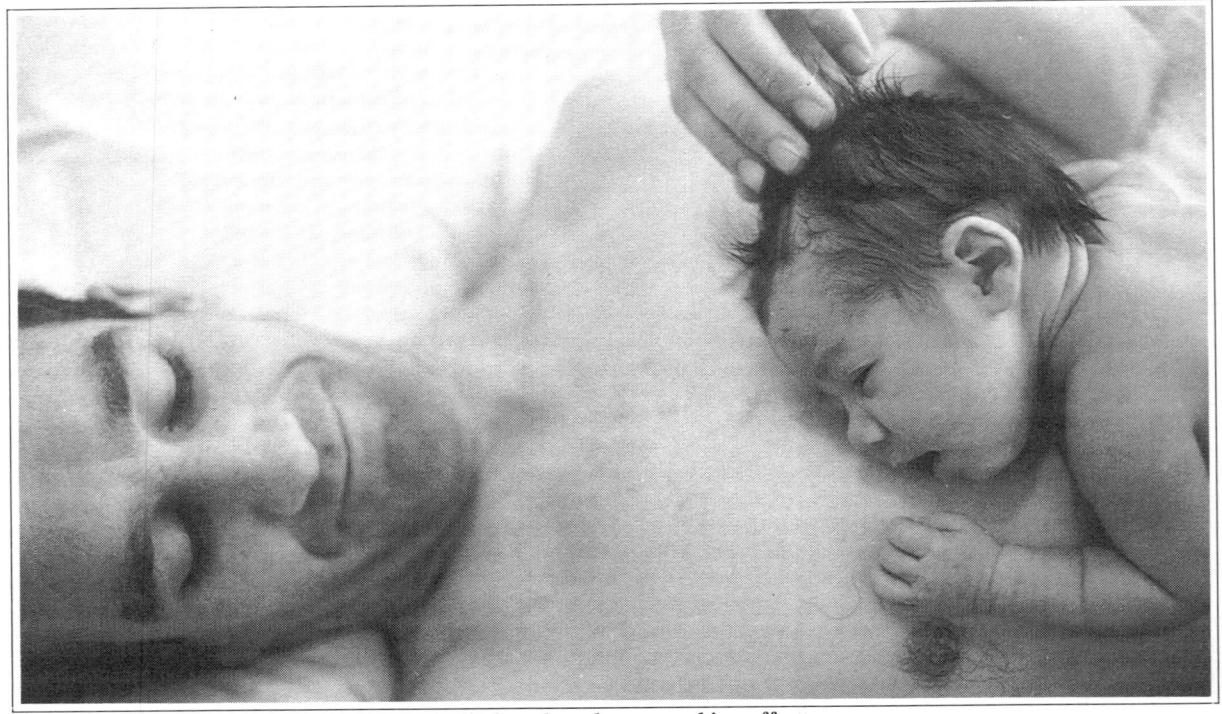

Dad's heartbeat has a soothing effect.

According to a study of crying charts, when the baby reaches the age of about 12 weeks he starts being sociable, happy and chattering at the very same time of the day he used to cry. It almost appeared that this crying period was the precursor of a sociable period. The end of these crying periods coincided with baby doing other, more interesting things such as cooing, smiling, babbling and so on . . .

CRYING IS NOT COLIC!

PROFESSOR Samuel Menahem, Associate Clinical Professor at the Royal Children's Hospital, says colic is a misnomer and a more appropriate term would be Infant Distress Syndrome.

The phrase was coined by Professor Wallace Ironside some years ago and it is gradually being used more frequently by the medical profession and others.

"True colic implies pain and we can't be sure about that," says Professor Menahem. "In many cases of crying babies, only a very few would suffer from medical things like bowel obstructions.

"To say all crying babies suffer colic only further increases the anxiety of parents who feel obligated to relieve the baby's so-called 'pain' rather than look and see what different factors may be contributing to the crying."

Sometimes new parents will hear people attribute a baby's crying to wind, but most evidence suggests wind is rarely the cause of crying — it may be the baby is hungry or just wants some comfort.

Professor Menahem, with Dr David Hill, has conducted a study into the significance of allergies in a baby's crying patterns. Part of the study involved a cry chart to observe both what the baby did and how the parent responded.

"We recorded the crying of so-called normal and so-called colicky babies," said Prof Menahem. "There has already been quite a difference shown in the amount they cry. We then select the crying ones and vary their diet, whether they are bottle or breast fed."

Some professionals believe diet and allergies play a big role in crying babies, but Prof Menahem says his own feeling is that it would be only a very small group.

However, Sandy Jones, in her book *Crying Baby, Sleepless Nights,* says it has been clearly demonstrated that a breastfeeding mother's diet can affect her baby, especially if he is sensitive to certain allergens.

Mothers can conduct their own tests for food allergies by eliminating each suspected food from their diet, one at a time, to see if your baby becomes less fussy. You can recheck by introducing the eliminated food again to see if it causes irritability or crying. Breastfeeding mothers should be careful not to eliminate certain foods, particularly milk, without replacing its nutrients.

Professor Menahem says the Melbourne study was the first time the responses of the parents had been documented which he believed was an important consideration. "If the mother comes and says the baby has colic, doctors tend to work at ways of treating the so-called pain but that eliminates so many other causes of the crying without even finding out why they are crying.

"It is important to remember babies who do have true colic because of bowel obstructions go quite limp and look very sick. Colic implies that there is a muscle contraction and that implies pain. It is better to look at other reasons for the crying."

Prof Menahem says colic, or Infant Distress Syndrome, is not uncommon and studies show that crying may be a normal physiological function.

> **HELPFUL HINT**
> Dummies, unfortunately, have a bad name and yet many parents have saved their sanity by using one of the numerous shapes and varieties available today. As one top paediatrician commented, dummies and other baby and child comforters really are a "non-issue". If it works for the baby and gives you peace then go for it!

One study showed that of 80 normal infants followed and studied at six weeks of age, the median duration of crying was 2.75, or nearly three, hours per day. The differences between "colicky" and normal infants thus became either arbitrary or based simply on the incidence of sudden paroxysms of crying.

"The only definite statements one can make is that 'normal' babies cry for two or three hours per day at six weeks of age for reasons that are far from clear," says Prof Menahem. "This is not usually relieved by the infant being picked up and no physical abnormality can be found."

Prof Menahem says a number of studies of infant colic have failed to demonstrate any definite correlation with age of mother, sex of infant, family history of allergy, type of feeding, amount of gas in abdomen or frequency and nature of bowel actions.

He says one study found a significantly higher number of first born infants suffering colic, but others did not.

"Apart from problems of definition, there are two other confounding factors," he says. "One is the interactional nature of the problem and the other, spontaneous improvement in the affected infants at 12 to 16 weeks," he says.

The stress and anxiety that comes with a crying baby is highlighted by Jenny's experience and as many other mothers have suggested:

The response from the medical profession is very often unrealistic and seemingly uncaring.

The parents say they feel they are "exaggerating the problem", that they are looking for easy ways out and they are not given much credibility in diagnosing their baby's problems.

According to Prof Menahem, a validated observation crying diary needs to be used to provide more objective data to define the crying and to assist doctors. He says this would result in a more reliable method for defining and studying colic than relying on parental description of duration and severity of symptoms. It seems that because the problem (the crying) seems to improve with time, it is difficult to know what the so-called successful interventions are and if, in fact, they do what they are said to do.

Prof Menahem says there are four main theories which may account for colic:

- The transmission of allergies in breast milk or the effect of food substances such as egg or cow's milk.

- Abnormal intestinal peristalsis or excessive amounts of gas in the abdomen causing gaseous distension and colic.

- Increased sensitivity to internal and external stimuli.

- Maternal anxiety, leading to increased infant crying. Mothers should try not to make too much of this, nor feel "guilty" if they are anxious around their babies as it is possible that all these factors are operating in some way.

Prof Menahem says maternal anxiety as a precipitating cause of colic has been a controversial issue over the past 40 years.

"There appears to be two separate issues," he says. "First, whether anxiety in the mother can cause colic in itself, and second, whether an infant's crying induces anxiety in the mother, which subsequently increases colic.

"In recent years there has been justifiable hostility from many mothers who are angry at being made to feel neurotic, inadequate and subsequently dependent by what they argue is misinformation about the role of anxiety in causing colic."

He says the most appropriate conclusions to be drawn

Illustration by Chris Fisher

from studies so far are that maternal anxiety may indeed affect infant behavior and certainly does affect the mother's perception of the infant's behavior, but that it is simply one added stress on the infant. More careful and precise studies of the relationship of maternal anxiety and infant colic are required.

There is no evidence that maternal anxiety is the cause of colic.

Many mothers related to me that they knew when they were getting uptight — after four nights of constantly interrupted sleep they admitted they were showing signs of emotional decay and "maternal anxiety". One mother said she learned to take a deep breath and walk away for a short while to calm herself down. "What I did was count to 50 and then slow down my movements so that I was patting the baby instead of banging and I was whispering in a soothing voice instead of pleading," she said.

"Another trick was to stare at her and close my eyes. During the day, the best answer to our stress was to go for a walk. All that activity soon tired the baby out and gave me something else to think about, like how lucky I was to be out picking flowers and not cooped up in an office building somewhere . . ."

Prof Menahem says infant colic is best described as the end result of a complex set of interactions between the infant and his environment, with environmental stimuli and stresses acting on an infant's immature nervous system.

He says the commitment of the medical profession should be to providing a nurturing environment for the infant by supporting the parents, encouraging expressions of doubts and anxieties, and the provision of practical hints and information.

Prof Menahem says that the management of crying could first include a simple physical examination perhaps by a local doctor. Parents should exclude any abnormality or illness and then make sure the baby is not underfed because crying often occurs because of hunger, he says.

"The next thing is to explain the crying to the mother as well as offer reassurance — that management doesn't mean you have to do something every time the baby cries.

"Some parents feel they can't let the baby cry at all. If you can't, and need a break, let someone else take over for a while.

"Parents, mothers especially, should get support and some relief especially if they are tired and depressed. Medicines sold over the counter often have a sedating effect, but very few babies should need it.

"The other advice is to let them cry — if you have done all you can then you should be reassured it is okay to let them cry."

I like to remember this advice so that I am able to enjoy the quiet times with my baby; the times he is most receptive to learning which really does begin from birth. Right from the beginning babies love to touch, feel and experiment. Turn your floor into your baby's classroom. Use the floor for playing, dressing and changing. Lie on the floor and investigate the world as he sees it. Try rolling, crawling, climbing and encourage his natural curiosity.

HOW TO STOP BABY CRYING

- *Try things like movement, bathing, walking, carrying, music or calming talk.*
- *Lay your baby on your chest so he can feel your heartbeat.*
- *Take comfort from the fact that crying babies are generally well, happy, healthy babies with nothing physically wrong with them.*
- *It is normal to feel angry, frustrated and helpless if you have a baby that cries for long periods — try and get a break.*
- *Do not be too proud to ask for help from professionals as well as friends.*
- *Accept that your baby will cry . . . so you can enjoy the quiet times.*

SECTION ONE

4

THE FAMILY BED
Make room for baby

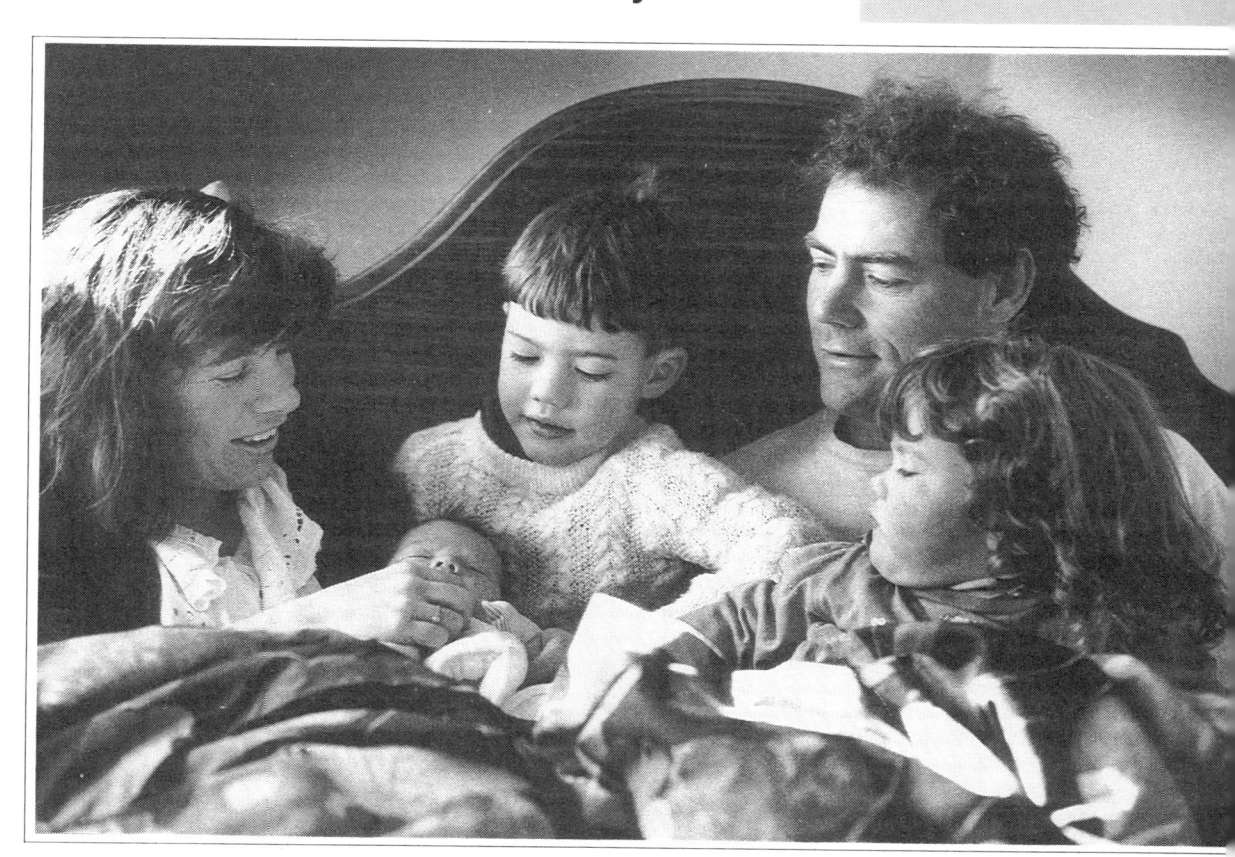

- *When baby won't sleep.*
- *Sleep deprivation and what it means for parents.*
- *Sharing your sleep and your bed.*

ASK new mothers what they need most and they will unanimously say "more sleep". Fathers, too. They don't long so much for a romantic night out as they do for six hours straight.

Lack of sleep can cause all sorts of problems — depression, burnout, marital breakdown, and of course a "low-functioning" brain — which is why we need it so much. It is a well-known fact that sleep deprivation is considered a very good brainwashing technique. But do our children know something we don't? Is it their way of getting parents to give in?

While some people need more sleep than others, no-one can last too long on only a couple of hours each night. Anyone who has ever been woken constantly in the middle of the night will know that horrible, groggy feeling. It is very hard to suddenly become alert and tune in, no matter how hard you try.

So all the best intentions — to remain relaxed, calm and caring when settling baby or child — can go out the window as soon as you are tired and unable to think clearly.

And when there is more than one child wanting your very "low-grade" night-time attention one after another, it is even harder.

Basically, when it comes to sleep we have two choices. We can take on 24-hour attachment parenting and let our young babies share our bed or keep them close by in their own bassinette and go to them whenever they cry. Or we can opt for the "tough it out" method which means letting them cry.

Paediatrician and author Christopher Green and other child behavioral experts call the latter the "controlled crying" technique which involves parents leaving the baby or child to cry. Most often they recommend it only after six months of age.

This method is certainly difficult initially and usually means several tense nights of letting the baby cry but most experts say it works

Parents are not so easily convinced, however, and some claim it actually makes settling the child more difficult and prolonged.

One of the most often asked questions of maternal and child health nurses is "when will my baby stop waking at night?". For those parents ticking off the days, the simple answer is "there is no magical age". It varies with each baby and child as they develop their own sleep pattern. They all go through different stages of sleep — Rapid Eye Movement (REM) sleep or "active sleep", deep sleep and "dream" sleep. The experts generally refer to the first two hours of sleep as deep sleep. When we start feeling tired, our body temperature decreases and as sleep becomes deeper our temperature continues to go down and if we are woken during our deep sleep we feel lousy.

This is because our nocturnal sleep cycle and our body temperature have reached their lowest point.

Depending on your child's reason for waking and his cycle of sleep, he could be easy or difficult to setttle. Although night feeds for me are now but a memory I am still tending to cries in the night and visitors to our bed. I do, however, consider myself very lucky when I hear some of the horror stories from mothers and fathers about sleepless nights that go on for months and sometimes even years.

So how about shared parenting? That's when it's truly put to the test. How many times have I tossed and turned waiting for Jon to hear the boys (but he doesn't) only to give him a less than gentle nudge. Admit it, we've all done it!

And how many new parents have sat through re-runs of *Star Trek* or *Here's Lucy* at 2am, trying to settle a crying baby . . . and still get up for the early, early starts?

HELPFUL HINTS

Consider "sharing sleep" or extending the family bed for your new baby. But never take baby to bed with you when drinking alcohol or taking sedatives. Do beware of overheating.

I like the idea of having babies in bed with me, especially new babies. When James and William were very young I would often feed them in bed and we would drop off to sleep together. I remember then always putting James back in his bassinette, but felt much more confident and comfortable with William staying in bed with me. Certainly, it is a difficult question as parents are faced with many theories and opinions on the subject of letting baby sleep with them.

A recent New Zealand study of SIDS found that babies who stayed in bed with their parents were at risk of overheating, a contributing factor in the condition according to some theories. And yet other studies found a baby was more settled and contented sleeping with its mother. This sort of thing is typical of much of the conflicting advice with which parents are faced. Parents should not place too much significance on all that they read or hear through newspapers and television.

The important thing is for parents to put it all into perspective, to filter the information and knowledge they glean from experts and friends and gain confidence in their own choices.

Of course, sharing your bed with a budding acrobat and then blaming your partner for that mysterious tap on the shoulder is a different story: "Leave me alone . . .". "It wasn't me, it was the kid!" When a child is sick or in need of special care and attention, sharing your sleep and your bed is often the natural thing to do.

ROOMING IN AND SHARING BEDS

ROOMING in, the hospital practice of babies remaining with their mothers 24 hours a day, may be extended to when you go home if it suits you and your family.

Certainly, the benefits of close contact with a new baby have been clearly demonstrated. Studies have shown that most babies settle better when they are near or with their mothers and mothers sleep better when they are close to their baby. It can also help with night feedings as the mother can breastfeed while resting in bed and therefore minimise the sleep loss and keep baby contented.

Mothers and babies sleeping together has been a way of life for centuries. However, Western countries rejected this world-wide natural custom during the last century only to find that today the benefits of sharing sleep or "bedding-in" are being considered more widely.

Of course, it may not suit all families. Some parents are scared of rolling onto the baby, or of him falling out of bed. Perhaps they could consider a "crib-in", which is attached to the bed and supported by a frame under the mattress. Alternatively, they can have the crib or cot beside their bed.

Staunch supporters of this "attachment" parenting and sharing of beds believe that if started early enough there may never be any sleep problems at all.

American paediatrician and Assistant Professor of Paediatrics at the University of Southern California, Dr William Sears, has written a book on night-time parenting, including the theory of sleep. He says parenting is much more than a full-time job — it goes on around the clock, 24 hours a day, and night-time is often the most difficult.

"In my own family we practice the concept of sharing sleep, a practice also known as the family bed, and I have advocated this co-sleeping arrangement to my patients," Dr Sears says.

"It works for most families most of the time. During baby's first year, mother and child share more than bed space; they also share sleep patterns.

"Sharing sleep may mean having your baby sleep in your bed next to you or in a sidecar arrangement with his cot next to your bed. If your child is older, it may mean a mattress on the floor alongside your bed."

Dr Sears says babies sleep better.

Sharing sleep helps babies as they pass from deep or quiet sleep into light or active sleep.

These vulnerable periods occur as often as once every hour during the night, he said.

Sleeping with a familiar and predictable person smooths the passage from one sleep state to the next and lessens the baby's anxiety. When a baby awakens partially during these vulnerable periods, the attachment person helps him resettle himself before he is fully awake. For older children, "attachment objects" such as a favorite doll or teddy or blanket help smooth the transitions from one sleep state to the next.

"Mothers sleep better," says Dr Sears. "It may come as a surprise but not only does baby sleep better in the family bed, most parents do also. Certainly mother usually does.

"Baby is not the only one who is separation sensitive at night. A new mother lies awake and wonders 'is my baby alright?' — the further away she is from her baby the deeper her anxiety.

"Physical closeness causes mother and baby to share sleep cycles; their internal clocks are synchronised with each other. Mothers who do achieve this synchronisation report that they feel rested."

CASE STUDY

FAMILY BED IN THE LIVING ROOM

MARIE says it was not until after her third child that she realised how great the family bed really was.

'It is much easier to get a lot of sleep with the baby in bed with you. As soon as I was able to, I took him to bed with me and while he slept I just stared at him in amazement. His siblings were there for the birth and because we were in a birthing centre they both climbed onto the bed with us while dad went to get drinks all round.

Just being so close to each other, our skin to skin contact, seemed to relax him and he slept soundly while we all celebrated his birth.

When we went home from hospital the next day we moved the new 'king size' family bed into the living room and it became the focal point of our lives for the next couple of months.

The baby sleeps through everything and his brother and sister never feel left out and I can honestly say there has been no jealousy or resentment of the new baby.

At night it is wonderful because as soon as I hear him stirring I feed him immediately and he is back off to sleep without my stirring too much. If he gets restless, I just pat his stomach or rock him and he settles.

The older children start off in the big bed and when they are asleep we take them to their own beds. My husband took a while to get used to the idea and he worries that people think we are a bit 'weird' but he is happy to be getting his sleep.

He was recently reassured by his own mother who said her mother, who had nine children, always slept with the newborn and her father slept in another bed with the older baby. The older kids had each other to comfort them.

I'm not quite sure how they managed nine children with these sleeping arrangements, but my guess is their interludes were all the more romantic for it.'

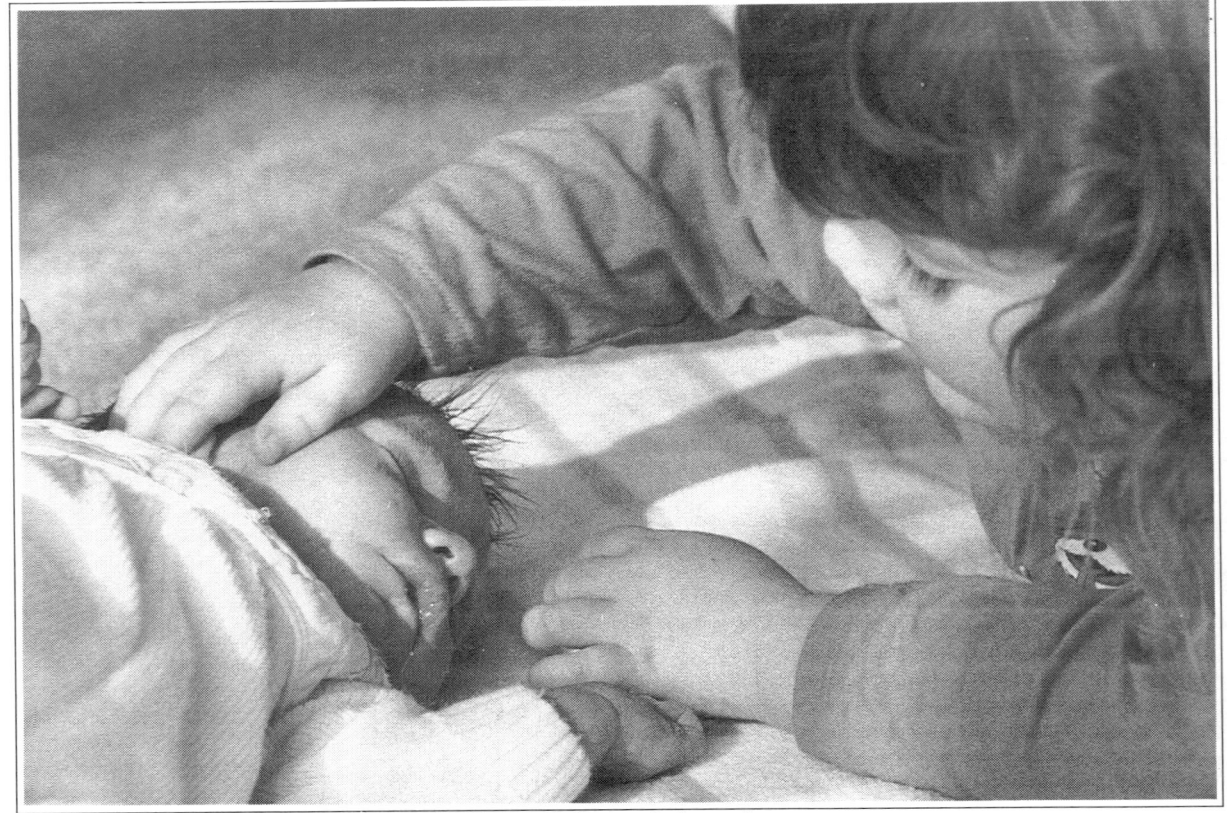

Big sister helps pat baby to sleep.

Dr Sears explains that when harmony in sleep is not achieved, night-time parenting becomes a reluctant duty. "Being awakened from a state of deep sleep to attend to a hungry and crying baby makes the concept of night-time parenting unattractive and leads to exhausted mothers, fathers and babies," he said.

He adds that when mother and baby's sleep cycles are in harmony, night-time feeding is less tiring. Mothers usually find it much easier to roll over and nurse than to get out of bed, go into another room, turn on a light, pick up a crying baby, locate a rocking chair and finally feed the baby. By this time both mother and baby are wide awake.

"Prolactin is the 'mothering' hormone and perhaps the chemical basis for mothers' intuition, and the three conditions that make the levels go up are sleeping, breastfeeding your baby and touching or simply being with your baby," Dr Sears says. "Sleeping with your baby allows all three of these conditions to occur."

Sharing sleep increases touching and can have a profound effect on how the baby develops. "The extra touching that a baby receives by sleeping with his parents definitely has a beneficial effect on his development," he says. "I suspect that infants who sleep with their mothers grow better, that babies thrive better when sleeping with their parents because of a combination of both nutritional and sensory inputs."

Dr Sears' survey of parents concerned about their children's sleep problems resulted in most parents reporting that their children slept better when sharing sleep.

"They awakened less often and experienced fewer nightmares and night-time disturbances," he says. "Co-sleeping helps children develop a healthy sleep attitude. They learn to regard sleep as a pleasant time, a time of closeness."

Dr Sears adds that psychologists agree that the quantity and quality of mothering does affect the emotional and intellectual development of the child.

"Extending the practice of daytime attachment parenting into night-time parenting does have long term effects on the child . . . psychologists report that many adult fears and sleep problems can be traced back to uncorrected sleep disturbances during childhood," he says.

Imagine it from the baby or child's point of view. In our society we prepare them for independence in a harsh way — beginning with night-time separation when we put them in a room by themselves, turn the light off, shut the door and leave.

It is only natural they will cry out from loneliness.

Despite the advantages, Dr Sears agrees some parents are still hesitant to adopt sharing sleep. The reasons he cites are usually cultural programming, misguided professional advice, the fear of what people will say and concern about dependency.

"Babies sleeping with parents is the usual custom in most cultures around the world and was common in the Western world until the 20th century," he said.

"Even today, mothers sleep with their babies but are afraid to tell their doctors or in-laws about it. These mothers are doing what their instincts tell them to do, but because of ridiculous social taboos they are made to feel uneasy about it. In my own survey, three out of four mothers favored sleeping with their babies.

"Experts on SIDS no longer list overlaying as one of the causes (of the syndrome) and mothers say they are so physically and mentally aware it is extremely unlikely.

"The occasional reports of overlaying are difficult to substantiate. It is interesting that the fear of SIDS is often given as one of the reasons why mothers do sleep with their babies."

Fears about diminished or ruined sex life are also unwarranted, according to Dr Sears and most of the parents I spoke to who shared their bed with their children.

The solution, they say, is to find more exotic places for lovemaking and to realise that a happy baby once fast asleep in his "shared bed" will wake for nothing but food!

Other concerns of parents tossing up between a shared bed and a bed of their own are "Will we all fit?" and "How long will it continue?" Some suggestions have been to attach a single bed to the double bed so the older child can gravitate to their own bed in their own good time. Or some parents keep a spare mattress on the floor by the bed for the midnight stalker!

Those who have let their babies and children sleep with them report the child eventually wants their own bed and does not associate bed with sleep trauma. Others have said sleeping with an older brother or sister has worked for the older baby.

CONTROLLED CRYING AND CHEATING

PSYCHOLOGIST and Director of the Australian Institute of Rational Emotive Therapy, Dr Robert Dawson, says most parents accept a new baby crying and not settling well but once the child gets a bit older they expect more mature behavior.

CASE STUDY

MY BABY WON'T SLEEP

KAREN calls her son a "cat napper" as he has never slept for more than half an hour at a time since he was born.

'As a baby, he would sleep for half an hour and be awake for three hours. He was happy when he was awake if you were with him, but if you left the room he cried.

I breastfed for about six months and initially it was on demand about every three hours. I accepted the lack of sleep then but when he got to five months and slept through the night for nearly a week I thought we had made it. But then he started waking again, once a night, twice a night.

It sounded like he was waking with a fright and then other times he was standing up in his cot ready to play. I didn't always go to him.

If he was only grizzling I left him but if he was left too long he would get hysterical. It took longer to settle him.

I started feeding him again with a bottle two or three times a night just to get him back off to sleep. It was all that worked.

The lack of sleep for his dad and myself nearly drove us crazy. I would get tired and irritable during the night but during the day I could manage until about four or five in the evening. That's when it would hit me. I tried controlled crying but Len couldn't stand it. He said he couldn't sleep while the baby was crying and he would give in too easily just for some sleep.

The one thing that did work for a while was to put him in the bouncer beside our bed and bounce him off to sleep. He would wake again in an hour or so.

It did put a strain on our marriage; we snapped at each other and couldn't be bothered having a conversation or going anywhere. I finally went back to work part-time when he was 10 months old and it's the best thing I ever did.

He is definitely an only child. If he had been an easy child I would have had more children but I couldn't take the chance of it happening all over again. It's too demanding. It doesn't concern me that he will be an only child.

I am the type of mum who is willing to listen to any advice and I would ask other people all the time what they thought, but most mothers I seemed to meet had terrific babies who slept!

I sometimes saw the battle as being more with my husband. It was hard to change him and we had to agree on what to do. Finally we went to a paediatrician. It gave us ideas but didn't solve anything. He just grew out of waking at night . . . when he was about three.'

He says that crying at bedtime is usually due to a child's fear of being deserted.

"The distress is about that fear, he can't know that mum will come back to him," says Dr Dawson. "When mum is out of sight she doesn't exist.

"So it could be one — fear — and two — he is simply not ready and three — he wants attention. All have to be dealt with rationally. Whatever it is you choose to do, you have to give the child the message you won't desert them. Parents tend to choose a bedtime that suits them and not the family.

"What does it matter if the child stays up until 10pm unless the parents are complaining about having no time together and needing that time to do other things? Personally, I think the child needs the sleep, but if it causes no problem for the child to stay up later and then goes to bed easier, then that is a decision for the parents.

"But for those who want them off at a certain time then they should set up a bedtime routine. Remember, nine out of 10 children will cry when you leave them."

Dr Dawson says parents might wish to have a night light on but he does not think one is necessary. "It may encourage fear or teach the child that being alone in the dark is something to be afraid of and noise and light make it harder to sleep," he says.

The rule for "controlled crying", according to Dr Dawson and supporters of this technique, is that when the child screams, you leave him. Depending on your will and how upset he is you can stay away from three to five minutes.

The parent then goes in and settles the child. If he is standing up and screaming, the parent lies him down and comforts him until he stops crying.

"During this time," says Dr Dawson "the parent tries not to talk too much or at all, to the child. They can convey love and caring without too much talking and giving them too much attention.

"The moment the child stops crying and is settled, the parent should leave. If the crying starts again, which it will for a while, leave them cry for longer — how much is up to you. Then go through the same brief procedure of settling. And so it goes on with each period of staying away getting longer.

"What the child eventually learns is mum or dad will come back. The first few nights the child may fall asleep out of exhaustion but then you should have success anything after three to 10 nights."

Dr Dawson admits some parents cannot cope with this method. They think the crying will have a traumatic effect on the child, but he believes there is no evidence to suggest it leads to long-term disturbances.

"The father maybe the stronger of the parents and he may have to help the mother not to go in and comfort all the time," he says. "For most parents, the realisation that their baby or child can cry and it has no bad side-effects occurs when the child is about 18 months of age but there is no fixed time. It just may be when the parent has had enough of crying at bedtime."

While good sleeping patterns are ideally established when the baby is very young — from as early as three months of age when the baby starts to distinguish between light and dark and routines like bathing, feeding and sleeping are taking shape — sometimes new problems arise for older children.

Toddlers often wake during the transition periods from light to deep sleep.

Routine again is vital and parents should take the extra time to establish regular calming activities before bedtime like bathing or a story in bed or a special quiet game. Jon is not allowed to leave the boys' room without the ritual "peace be with you" to which the boys reply "and also with you, my father"! And another all-time favorite is "sleep tight, don't let the bed bugs bite!"

Dr Dawson says there are some very specific "don'ts" associated with controlled crying and that if you get them wrong you may continue to have a problem.

"Don't give in," he says. "If, at the end of 15 minutes, mum thinks the child is so distraught that she can't do it any longer and takes the child out of the cot and feeds and cuddles and so on, the child will learn if he screams long enough and loud enough he will get what he wants. And the mother is back to where she started but worse off. The child will be prepared to go on for longer next time.

"You have to make a commitment to follow it through. If you can't handle it, stick to your own ways.

"Putting the child to bed somewhere other than their own bed and room may also cause problems. You should make

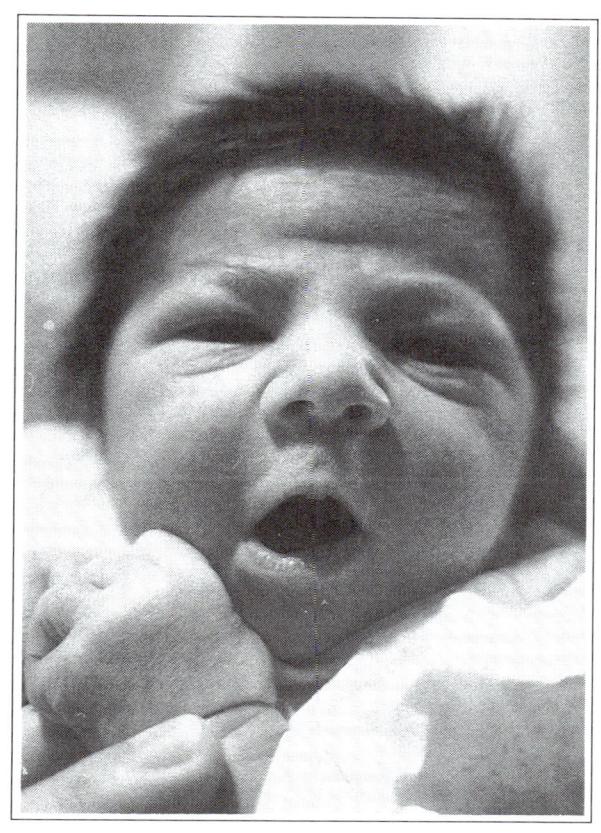

Sleeping like a baby?

(which should be medium — not too hot and not too cold) and warming and airing the bed regularly.

Another factor parents should consider is medical problems such as sleep apnea, which is basically a breathing difficulty. Parents can observe their child sleeping to see if there are problems and if they are concerned they should consult a doctor.

> ## HOW TO MAKE BAJY SLEEP
>
> • *Create sleep routines or bedtime rituals from a young age. Try baths, swaddling, lying down with baby, patting or "laying on hands".*
>
> • *Breastfeeding and rocking to sleep are good (but be wary of bottles and the damage sugar on the teats can do to baby's teeth).*
>
> • *Sounds of the womb, a sheepskin or special rug, a bed on wheels (pram) are good for inducing sleep.*
>
> • *If you have an early riser, let them know the rules about not waking anyone else (if they are old enough to understand) and try leaving a box of things for them to do.*
>
> • *Have set times for older children. An alarm may sound the time, or a bedtime story or a special game.*
>
> • *If you have tried everything, consider controlled crying — let them cry for a set time before comforting them, and keep increasing the time away from them.*

Allowances for the changed environment, but only to a point. The rules are the same, stagger the crying and comforting times.

"Don't be anything but boring when you go to the child, even anger is a reward to them. Sometimes the tugs a mother feels are so strong she finds it almost impossible to limit her interaction and that's where the father can support her. It is not that the mother is weak it's just that she is biologically tuned to baby's pain or she may even feel a failure."

Controlled crying will make going to bed worse before it gets beter, says Dr Dawson, and parents should be prepared for the child not to like it and even to become hysterical.

"The next advice then is how to cheat," he says. "We are all basically human and you can cheat by not waiting the full time out but by no other way. You should still say very little or nothing at all when you go in. If they struggle with you or won't lie down, walk out again. But don't cheat too much!"

Sometimes a child's sleep problems may be associated with things other than attention seeking or separation anxiety. Diet is an important factor in sleep. Bananas and milk are longtime favorites for inducing sleep. The environment is important, particularly the temperature of the room

SECTION ONE

5

LIFE CAN BE CRUEL
But it is always precious!

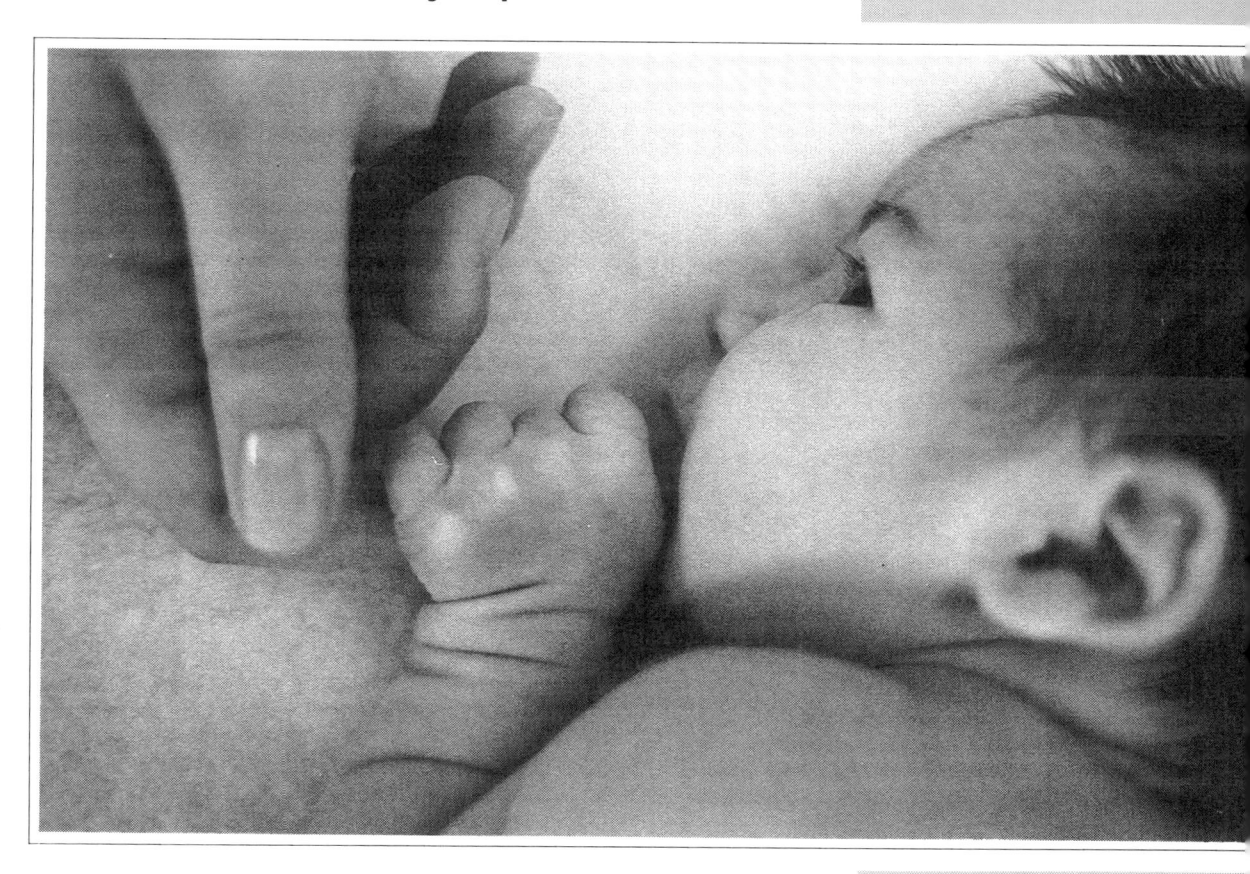

- Coping with the 'special needs' child (acute and chronic).
- The extra parenting of a child with special needs.
- The effects of sickness or disability on the family and siblings.

SOMETIMES it is not until a baby or child is sick that you realise how precious they really are. The love they give is often taken for granted or overlooked when coping with everyday survival.

Our first baby was not seriously ill but serious enough to need hospital care and attention. The time he was in hospital was long enough for me to gain some insight into the extra demands on parents of sick babies and children — those with acute, long-term and even life threatening illnesses.

I remember walking around the hospital watching mothers with blank, zombie-like faces snoozing in waiting rooms, keeping a constant vigil by their child's bed, or drinking coffee in the canteen just trying to cope. I could only imagine the incredible suffering they must be enduring.

Like them, I hated leaving my child alone and I phoned the hospital constantly to check on him. I felt so responsible — I should have been able to do more. If I could, I would have swapped places with him. I wanted to take away the pain and the suffering but I couldn't. And at home it felt so empty, no early morning wake-up cries and no toys to trip over.

Parents of premature babies or those born with rare heart conditions, disease or other complications say they experience many moments of self-doubt, anxiety and questioning. Many, however, say they go on to derive strength from the adversity or illness and some actually felt the whole family benefits from the experience.

As one mother observed: "Many of these experiences are what parenting is all about — it opens your eyes up to what life really is, shocks you out of your comfortable life and really challenges you to come to grips with it."

When there is a serious illness or disability in a family everyone has to make adjustments. The father may have to stay in a secure job rather than start his own business, or the mother may have to put her career on hold or reassess her ambitions in order to come to terms with the challenges of the sick baby or child.

Somehow the kids cope the best. During my time at the hospital I saw little children badly burnt, dying of cancer and enduring endless tests — but they all remained little children doing the things they loved.

Sometimes what they needed most urgently was a big hug.

Even when your baby or child has a cold, ear infection, high temperature or teething problems, as much as anything else they need comfort and a cuddle.

When my son was in hospital, I remember thinking "Why us? How could it happen?". But our drama was insignificant compared to those problems some parents and their children were forced to endure.

I was impressed, however, with Melbourne's Royal Children's Hospital and its philosophy of "completing the care" so that not only the sick children but mums, dads, brothers, sisters and grandparents are all looked after.

The hospital has a support network for families and Ronald McDonald House which accommodates families of sick children, especially those undergoing treatment for leukaemia or other life-threatening illnesses. I have heard of similar services both here and interstate and parents with children in hospital should seek out the range of services and help available to them.

Another important issue highlighted by many parents was their need to demand, and receive, information and support from professionals such as surgeons, social workers and nurses. Remember, it is their job to answer your questions and put you in touch with services available to you and your family.

Ronald McDonald House has a caring team of professionals, medical specialists, social workers, nurses, therapists, volunteers and teachers at the hospital school who help to make it a little less stressful. Sometimes the children themselves go to the house to convalesce and it helps to have familiar faces around them.

I discovered the most important thing about the house and other support services was that parents could relax and worry less about some of their everyday problems.

Ronald McDonald House and similar accommodation facilities available to parents of premature or seriously ill babies give families an opportunity to stay together. Previously one parent had to stay at home with the other children. Families from the country, interstate and even outer Melbourne often need accommodation to be near their children and motels can be expensive and sterile — although many would sleep on park benches if they had to.

Ronald McDonald House does not have formal counselling services but parents can, and do, talk among themselves. As I have learned, a family who can stick together through a crisis can make it through the situation much easier. Sometimes trauma may even bring them closer together.

PARENTING PLUS FOR SPECIAL NEEDS CHILDREN

Professor Gill Parmenter, head of the University of Melbourne's School of Early Childhood Studies, says sick or handicapped children do bring special demands to parenting.

"When a child is sick their demands for attachment and comforting are increased and to some extent they may even regress," Dr Parmenter says. "For a short illness the problems then arise of how to phase out that extra care and attention that has been required.

"For the long term ill or handicapped the real issue is one of independence.

The natural thing to do is to nurture and pamper and do almost everything for the child.

But there is a danger of the parent becoming overprotective and not fostering the child's independence."

Dr Parmenter says the other problem parents needed to be aware of was the effects of the illness on siblings. "If the parents' time and attention is focused on the sick child the other children are likely to feel left out," she says. "Sometimes it is just the physical demands of keeping doctors' appointments or if it is a demanding crying child, just keeping order.

"What they really should try to do is have special time for each of the other children. It's a bit like having a new baby, parents make sure the other children do not feel left out."

One way parents can give their other children special time is to have a support network, ideally family such as grandparents. But if they are not available, the local council or family services centre may be able to provide information about occasional care or home help or even a group for siblings.

Dr Parmenter says parents need to show all the children in the family that they are accepted for what they are and recognise each others' strengths and weaknesses. If a child is sick or disabled the disability is accepted. Parents can best do that by example.

"If the child and the siblings see that the parents are worried or anxious about it they will be too," she says. "Sometimes children who are sick or handicapped can actually derive strength from it which the rest of the family can benefit from. It can be a source of strength, but it does depend on the individual. Another child may be anxious and worried about it and what it does to their parents. The more the child can be helped to cope with it by themselves and take responsibility the better, if it is appropriate.

"What is particularly important for pre-schoolers is the parents' understanding of the child's experience."

Parents really do have to try and view it through the child's eyes.

If the child is upset or frightened by their illness or are afraid of doctors or hospitals, parents do need to encourage the child to talk about their fears.

"Pre-schoolers are not just inexperienced versions of

CASE STUDY

A GRATEFUL FATHER KEEPS HOPING FOR LIFE

KEVIN and his family have survived the tragedy of watching a little girl close to death recover. His two-year-old daughter was suffering from a malignant tumor but with special care and determination she fought it, even though there were times when he didn't know if she would make it.

'Sharing your fears and hopes with other parents and learning from the sick kids themselves is the best therapy. Some parents talk of hope, some of the multiple side-effects, some of the waiting for test results and still others of the successes.

Initially it is hard to believe what has happened — one night a normal life, the next, agonising uncertainty. Will my child live? There are tests, so many tests. Doctors tell you the results, tell you its cancer, cystic fibrosis, life sucking polyps or another condition you thought other children got, not your child. How could this happen?

So we gratefully stay at McDonald House when chemotherapy or a radiation treatment is required, or when our sweet child is having her operation and a longer stay is necessary. Some nights here a few of us sit together and talk about the treatment, about anything really. Everything is taken a day at a time, especially in the first week when it seems so unreal.

Gradually, the sharing of a common state bonds us a little as treatment effects begin — stomach aches, nausea, ulcerated mouths and so on. Your poor child is suffering, all you can do is comfort her, as nurses and doctors do their utmost to return your child to health.

Many a parent sleeps badly, preferring to be with their darling if needed during the night. When we can, we walk across the road and talk over tea and coffee and relax. Sometimes there is a crushing sadness about the place, sometimes enormous joy; often it feels like a comfortable community house.

A family might be returning home with little hope, little time to create new memories knowing that that is all there will be soon. At times it seems so insufferable, cruel, so hard to cope.

Our family is one of the happy ones. After the most magnificent care and professional expertise our little fighter is likely to be cured. All along we hoped and felt the best might well happen. For all the others who are trying to cope with childhood cancer, please keep on hoping, try to maintain your own and your child's determination.

Sometimes our hopes are ripped apart, yet we should continue to hope; amazing changes do occur. There is of course a terrible conflict in hope; we can hope for the best, while hoping itself is not going to bring rewards; so why hope? Because without hope there is hopelessness — we may as well blow up the world now.

We do not though. Life is at times too cruel but it is always precious.'

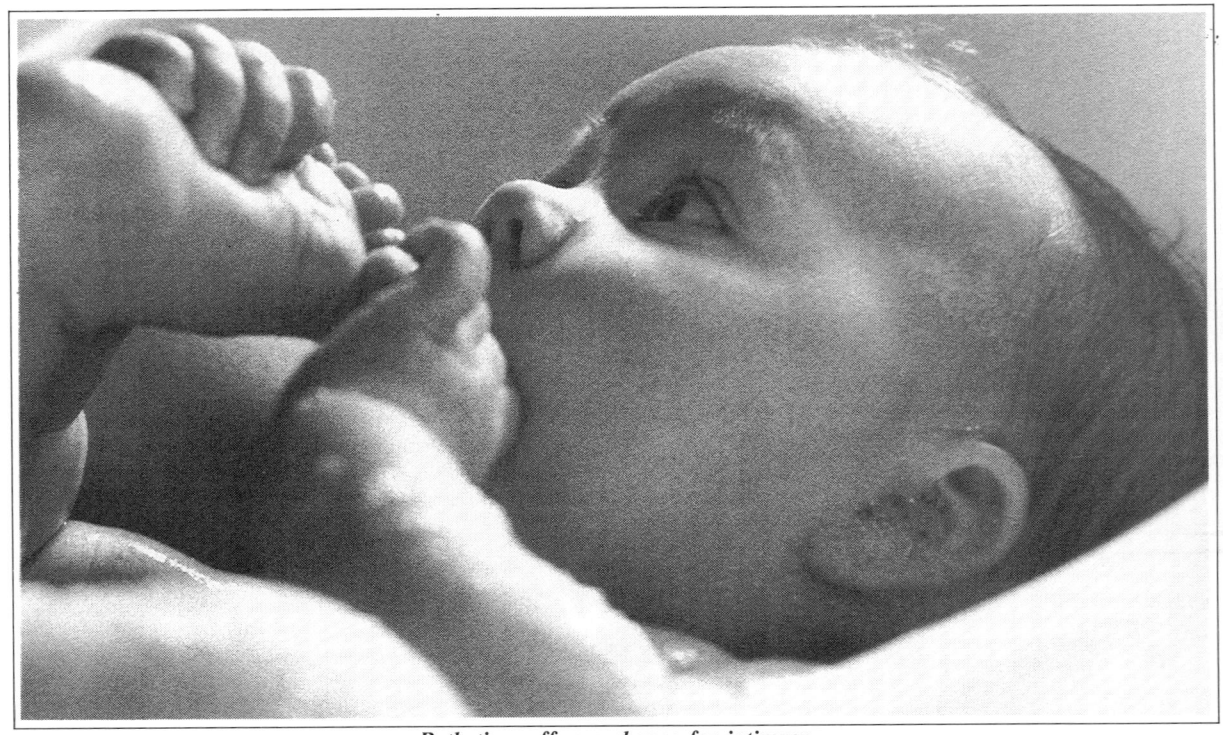

Bath time offers a chance for intimacy.

adults. Their ways of understanding events are often very different from ours and fears arise when we would have none (and vice versa). Parents need to acknowledge the child's fears, try to understand what the child is thinking and feeling and give help and support and explanation."

Dr Parmenter says that if an illness or handicap continually dominates the whole family, parents should consider relief care. "Everyone in the family is entitled to their own special time and if it means a short period of child care then it should be sought," she says.

TAKE ONE STEP AT A TIME AND GET SOME SUPPORT

THERE may be a clear-cut moment when you discover your child is disabled or perhaps the knowledge is a slowly-dawning realisation, but the expectations for you and your child and your family appear to change forever, write authors and mothers Anne Whaite and Judy Ellis in their book *From Me to You . . . Advice for Parents of Children with Special Needs.*

Some parents say instead of saying "why me?" to ask "why not me?". And some parents say they wish their baby would die. "Wishing your baby would die is not the same as wishing to harm your baby," say the authors. "It is a way of wishing that the problem and consequently the pain would go away. Remember that the future cannot be spelled out for you or for your child. You can only take one step at a time.

"Talking to relatives and friends about it may be difficult but if you can acknowledge what has happened straight away and tell people the things you feel you can talk about and those you can't, it may help. There are services for your son or daughter. While some of the more specialised ones may be difficult to find, or have long waiting lists, services are available for your child who has a disability. It is vital that all decisions are based on knowledge and information".

If the services are not available parents need to become involved with establishing them.

They should put pressure on members of parliament, form self-help groups and visit the library to get the latest information here and overseas. It is all part of empowerment for parents.

Many parents still meet professionals and others who give advice on disabilities based on their own attitudes rather than what is necessarily best for them or their child.

"Because it is so difficult to sort out what you are going to do, it is best to talk to as many informed people as possible," say the authors. "At the very least make sure you get a second opinion. Early education or early intervention is not a cure for your child's disability, but it does allow individuals to develop as much as possible, as soon as possible."

Unfortunately there are not nearly enough of these services available.

Assessment is an important step where a trained team of

medical and non-medical people try to find a diagnosis, or if a diagnosis has already been made to assess your child's development. "Assessment is not just to tell you what your child is not doing; it is to tell you the things that your child can do and to decide what is required to assist in overcoming any delay or difficulty," write Whaite and Ellis.

The book suggests that one of the biggest advantages of early education is that it helps to develop skills which will assist your child when it comes to attending ordinary pre-schools and schools. Early education can be home-based with regular visits by professionals, or centre-based where you take your child to a therapy centre, a clinic or a playgroup. The people running these services work as a team and can be special education teachers, physiotherapists, speech therapists, occupational therapists, play group leaders and sometimes social workers.

Early education programs nearly always involve parents working with their children at home and going back to a centre regularly for review and advice on what to do next.

This is the best possible partnership for the development of a child — parents and professionals working together.

There are a growing number of ordinary playgroups and pre-schools which enrol children with disabilities and many parents, while apprehensive at first, have found that the experience is very rewarding.

Children receive the greatest benefit in integrated settings when a special educator visits the playgroup or kinder on a regular basis, according to the authors. This gives the staff some assistance with programs, material and equipment.

Discovering services in the early years of your child's life may tax your patience and staying powers, but the effort is worthwhile.

"Contact with professionals is an inevitable part of life if you have a child with a disability," the book explains.

CASE STUDY

MIRACLES CAN HAPPEN

WHEN Jan gave birth to her first little girl she was delighted, but within 24 hours Sarah was rushed by a neonatal emergency ambulance to the Royal Children's Hospital with congenital heart disease. For the next six months Jan battled to keep her baby alive and at one time, after heart surgery, she and her husband faced decisions that meant Sarah would die.

❛I think I could face losing her but I could not handle saying 'okay, today is the day she is going to die' which was what had been suggested to us. If we felt it was too much for her we could just ask for an injection, we were told.

There were some doctors who were cold and matter-of-fact and there were some wonderful surgeons and cardiologists who were always there, anytime of day or night, to respond to an emergency. They really do save lives everyday.

When I was first told Sarah might not make it through I was crying, but after that there was not a lot of time for tears. Some mechanism inside just makes you cope day by day. The paediatrician told me I should cuddle Sarah but I was afraid to; I'm glad we did but there were not many times in those early weeks when we could bond.

The other thing that was hard was relatives and friends not sending cards when she was born. They had heard things weren't too good and didn't send cards. It felt like she had never been born.

There is a sense of grief because you have a baby but she is not with you. At one time I even thought 'well, why didn't I just have a miscarriage, why come this far to lose her?' I think I swayed between 'that's it' and then an inner calm that 'it would be alright'. I did wonder whether there really was a God. I was bitter.

At home we coped okay but we had to live in isolation because Sarah could not catch a cold and feeding was quite difficult. I chose to express because she needed my milk but I had to learn how to feed her through a tube which I had to put in her nose and down her stomach. Then there was the pumping of mucus that had to be done.

One of our worst periods was when Sarah was two months old and they discovered her heart problems were complicated by a lung condition.

I was very angry and upset this time because I had not been told. I started crying but I was on my own.

Then to make it worse I had one doctor telling me it was hopeless for Sarah and I just had to decide when she should die.

We just felt we had to give her a chance. She came off the ventilator and improved from there. My older boys have most definitely benefitted and grown from the whole experience. They have never been jealous of the time we have had to devote to their sister and they have shared in every achievement she manages.

They keep you going and they keep things in perspective. Sarah is special in that she is delightful and as the cardiologist assured us 'her brain is good'. She's busy catching up on the time she missed when she was so desperately ill and while there are still problems — like asthma — we are getting back to as normal a life as possible. ❜

HELPFUL HINT

A new booklet that is now available to parents of disabled children will certainly help many parents in their quest to improve services for their child and for their families. This practical guide to steer families in the right direction has been written by a group of mothers of disabled children.

The book shares the experiences, isolation and frustrations and occasional successes of parents and aims to make services more accessible and better co-ordinated.

"Helping Parents Help Themselves" shows how parents can contribute to the delivery of services and work as partners with professionals. It is a unique project not only because the words are those of the parents but also because it brings together the resources of health, education and community services under the umbrella of the Specialist Child and Family Services Program of Co-ordination.

Both professionals and parents need to work to establish good communication with each other. You may need to become more assertive in order to obtain the information and help that you need. Remember that professionals have a job to do and a responsibility to do it properly.

Remember you have rights — ask questions, ask for explanations and don't take no for an answer.

Most parents agree that the most effective source of information and support is other children who have disabilities. Seeking out other parents is not an admission of failure or inadequacy but it can be a really hard step to take.

As one mother of a little girl with Down syndrome says, the family's lifestyle is certainly different but she believes her other children are better off for learning to cope with it.

The mother says she experienced some very difficult times early on and there were days where she awoke and wished her daughter was not there: "I thought of SIDS and as much as I hate to say it I wished it would happen to my baby. Fortunately, that feeling passed and I have come to love her dearly. Going back to work and getting outside help has been good for the whole family."

SIBLINGS AND THEIR NEEDS

CHILDREN have a right to their thoughts and feelings and all you can do is acknowledge these as they arise, advise the experts.

"If they talk about how they feel towards their disabled brother or sister, don't ever say they shouldn't feel that way. Letting them talk about it will help them," suggest the authors of *From Me to You.*

"Information is as important for children as it is for adults. Without realistic information, children may form their own conclusions which could be highly distorted. Many parents feel that there should be more help and support for brothers and sisters. Some community workers are now establishing 'sibling groups' for older children.

"As society's awareness of the needs of people with disabilities and their families slowly grows, more of the responsibility is being shared by the community and more services are being provided. If you have a child with a disability you have a right to these services."

Children need to be encouraged and allowed to talk about things and they need time and help to incorporate problems in their play and drawings. The things that are left not discussed when adults are young are often those that give them the most anxiety later in life.

WAYS TO GET HELP

- *Learn to communicate with professionals to get the best possible help and when necessary seek a second opinion.*

- *Be assertive in your demands for the services your child, your family or your neighborhood may need.*

- *Consider joining a parents' support group as a way of keeping up with new ideas and sharing your experiences.*

- *Seek out the services in your area from early childhood learning centres to local playgroups that encourage integration.*

- *If the services are not available in your area or region form an action group to get them.*

- *Respite care is essential for you, your partner and your children.*

SECTION ONE

6

SHE'S JUST LIKE HER FATHER
Moody, shy, brilliant!

- *Babies arrive complete with their own personalities.*
- *Types of temperament — fussy, easy, demanding.*
- *Effects of child temperament on parenting style and ability to cope.*

WHEN couples first learn they are having a baby, the dreams and expectations that rush through their minds are often unrealistic.

It's called "image making" and refers to the preconceived ideas of what our baby will look like and what "kind" of baby we will have. For many those dreams are shattered when the "tiny" baby they imagined weighs in at 5 kilos or the "cuddly" bundle they pictured is premature and is no bigger than the parents' hands.

It is often hard to reconcile parents' hopes and dreams when the much hoped-for placid, smiling and well-nourished baby turns out to be quite fussy, crying and difficult to feed.

It is widely agreed that no two children are alike. Every baby is different and it is their very uniqueness that makes them special.

A child's temperament or personality/makeup is considered a very important aspect when dealing with behavior and development.

Like other changes in the management of our own health where we consider the whole person (the psychological aspects of any illness as well as the medical symptoms), parents and doctors must also take into account the "whole" child. Health professionals are encountering more and more problems related to children's behavior such as eating problems or sleep disturbances that have no apparent physical condition or illness as their basis.

I was aware that there were certain "types" of temperament and soon found my first son James fell into the "category" of easy, adaptable but ACTIVE. The capital letters stand for the attention an active child demands and it means he is into everything (which I'm told is better than not being into anything). But with James I also felt he was flexible — he could cope well with changes in routine, probably because he was the one setting the agenda!

With this insight into child temperament and acknowledging that all children are different, I admit I was somewhat apprehensive during my second pregnancy for what our second child would be like . . . difficult, inflexible, bored? William, I am pleased to report, was more of the same and if feeding and sleeping habits are to be marked he was closer to 10 out of 10. He was the "good" baby, the textbook one that makes parenting easy and fun. But what does that say about those that don't fit the "good" tag? They are not "bad" just more demanding. But as those parents of difficult babies concede, they love them every bit as much — they just require more work.

Second and subsequent babies are often described as being "easier". Perhaps it is because parents have now over-

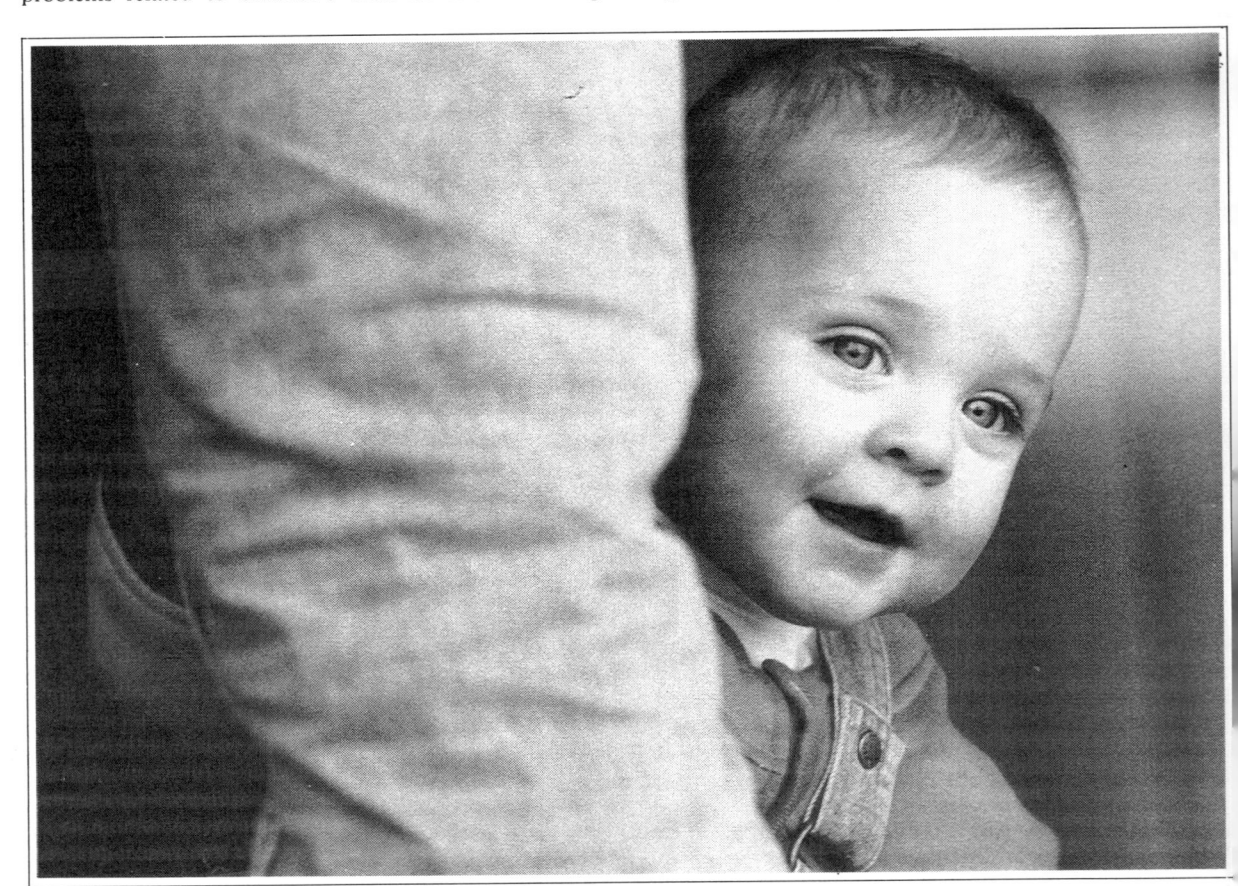

The "good" baby that makes it all fun.

come all those fears of the first-time round like: "Will he be okay? How do I know he is getting enough milk? Is he too hot, too cold, sleepy, hungry" and so on.

It is very hard for new parents to be sure that crying is not caused by health problems.

It seems we are always trying this remedy or that technique and just when we get used to one stage, the baby has moved onto another — or we've found a way of dealing with a problem and before you know it it's over!

When I mentioned this new found confidence and absence of anxiety with my second baby to a wonderful midwife nursing me at the Royal Women's Hospital, she assured me "you really will enjoy your second baby without the worry of the first . . . every baby should be a second baby".

While my boys do have a number of similarities, there are most definitely obvious differences. While James loves any sport — football, cricket, basketball, and now tennis lessons — William will be interested only for a while (as much for acceptance as anything I guess). William can happily amuse himself for long periods and while James is shy with attention William relishes the limelight! Other special qualities starting to shine through are his nurturing interests — he is the one who looks after the pets, making sure they are not hungry or thirsty.

I suppose this part of temperament or personality has as much to do with environment as biological makeup. By that I mean the child's need to find a place to belong in the family. Many psychologists see this as a child's most important and basic need.

While a child's personality will help determine the way they are and the way they act, their environment will influence their choices. You just have to look at your own family and others to see the evidence — where one child is good at sport the other will try for academic or musical achievement and a third might be the actor or the clown of the gang.

Temperament is an important consideration for parents

CASE STUDY

I COME FIRST, THE KIDS SECOND

MARIE says she has always stuck to the philosophy that her babies and children should have to fit in with her lifestyle and in that way she could enjoy motherhood.

'That attitude raises a lot of eyebrows but I've tried to keep to that. I was very lucky with the first baby who was a placid child and I only ever saw her throw one tantrum. I really think it's nature rather than environment that determines their personality.

We thought having babies was so simple we decided to have another, but number two was different. He was aggressive, he wanted things immediately and he screamed when he didn't get what he wanted. He was difficult to feed, difficult to satisfy and was a poor sleeper.

He turned out to be a bad asthmatic which may have been why he was such a difficult baby. It wasn't until he was two years old when he nearly died from an attack that we even discovered he suffered from it.

Our two kids were dragged everywhere, but at bedtime when the door was shut that was it. There was no more going to them. I have to confess I didn't believe in feeding during the night after a certain age, about six weeks . . . I was very much influenced by a friend of mine who had had nine children and she claimed that after the third one she stopped going to them in the night, she felt it was crying for attention rather than need.

So with that knowledge, I became very hard. It worked for all of my kids except the second one who we got up to five times a night until he was five years old, but it was because of his health, not for attention.

I haven't found that having four kids is easier or more difficult than one. But you do learn not to be as fussy and to take shortcuts. I pureed everything for my first child and my last one wouldn't know what it meant. Of course, you do gain a certain amount of confidence the more you do it. You learn the baby isn't going to die if it screams for a while and that you can leave it.

A baby doesn't have the same expectations as a toddler and I found the older child was the one wanting my attention and feeling put out. For Amy, my last, I always sat and fed her and that was our special time. You really try and make them fit in whereas with the first you tend to be a slave to them.

They've all been different. We never struck the 'good' one again. Our second is still quite aggressive, the third fairly placid but can throw a major tantrum, the fourth is a bit of a whinger. Maybe because she is the baby of the family, but she has always clung to me whereas the others didn't.

They have four very different personalities, none are the same although they have all had the same treatment. I know that with each child my temperament became more edgy but ultimately it came back to their own personalities and temperament.'

when coping with babies, toddlers and children in everyday events. A baby that is fussy and demanding will react differently to a situation than one who settles easily. Similarly, an anxious toddler will not feel good about his mother leaving him, or the demanding pre-schooler will be the one disrupting the kinder class.

One of the ways parents can assist their child through difficulties is to be aware of the child's personality and how they might react to things. James, I believe, is by nature determined and competitive but at times I see glimpses of a low-frustration tolerance. While he tries so hard to achieve, he can become angry if things don't go his way. How do we handle that? When he was younger we tried to ignore the yells of frustration and encouraged him to keep trying. Now he is older we can talk about it being worthwhile just to have a go. James also enjoys a good laugh. I don't know if that's temperament or just a sense of humor. But above all, James is super sensitive; he is deeply hurt when disciplined in front of people or when he feels let down by others.

William, on the other hand, already has this inner contentment; can cope with bullying from an older brother and nothing seems to frazzle him. "He's just like his father". Sometimes it seems like he is in a dream world and in that way he is very accident prone!

It could be easy to underestimate William's needs because of his easy temperament.

But as he gets older, the demand for special time has become more obvious. He does not compete with his older brother but rather seems to be looking for his own special interests. Other parents have talked of their hopes that each child will find something they are good at and enjoy doing. In the same way, a difficult child or a child with sudden mood changes will be harder for a parent to handle. Parents can often fall into the trap of not giving that child enough time and the relationship could be in danger of breaking down.

Parents are being told that they need to be aware of the biological function of temperament so they don't put themselves down and realise they don't have total control over the child. But some parents are in danger of taking it too far, believing nobody has the right to influence anyone else, including their children. Psychologist Jim Bates seem to have the right approach in his book *Becoming a Complete Parent*. He suggests parents not only have a right but a responsibility to influence, and even mould, their children.

Children do not live in a vacuum and as they will always be influenced by others it may as well be a nurturing and caring parent that helps to guide them.

PERSONALITY WILL AFFECT THE WAY A CHILD BEHAVES

THE Director of Ambulatory Paediatrics at the Royal Children's Hospital, Dr Frank Oberklaid, says a child's temperament can be considered a sort of filter through which they interact with the environment. It represents part of the child's unique individual makeup and must be taken into account by parents and teachers when dealing with a child, he says.

Child rearing practices and teaching styles need to be flexible enough to adapt to a child's temperament in order to promote a positive behavioral outcome, says Dr Oberklaid.

"Certain temperament characteristics, especially in the face of a rigid and insensitive environment, can predispose a child to behavioral and adjustment problems.

"All parents can testify that no two children are alike in terms of their temperament and personality. They differ in energy and activity level, in their reactions to new events and different life situations, and in a host of other qualities. Even in children from the same family, with the same parents and where one would expect most of the factors in the child's environment to be the same, we see significant differences between children."

Dr Oberklaid says that parents will often say that these individual differences are noticeable from birth and tend to endure; others say they change as the child gets older — but the term temperament is now often used to describe these differences.

"It is only in the last 20 years that children's temperaments or individual differences have been widely studied and generally accepted by the professional community," he says. "Prior to that time it was assumed that the child was passive in his reaction with the environment, and that any differences as he got older were due to differences in his environment.

"As a result there was a lot written about the best way to rear children, the assumption being that if parenting was good and the environment appropriate then a good outcome was assured."

Temperament has become an important tool for understanding the "how" rather than the "why" of behavior — the behavioral style of the child. While temperament is believed to be intrinsically determined, it also can be modified by the environment.

If parents who have children with difficult temperaments can find ways to make their environment more suitable, they may find it easier to cope. For example, the baby that does not sleep well because he is always active may need some help from the parents or carer to bring down the level of activity, to introduce quiet times like music or walking and rocking that will create an environment for sleep.

Part of the Australian study by Dr Oberklaid and collaborators from the Royal Children's Hospital and La Trobe University has confirmed studies from overseas which have demonstrated an association between the child's temperament and things like colic, sleep problems, excessive crying, temper tantrums, accidents, child abuse, school adjustment and other important areas of a child's functioning.

Dr Oberklaid says it is not the child's temperament alone which is important, but rather the interaction of those temperament characteristics with the environment. It is the manner in which a child's individual characteristics fit in with the child rearing style and attitudes of the parents which determine whether or not there will be behavior or other problems, he says. This theory supports the notion of a "goodness of fit" discussed in the section on bonding.

An infant with a difficult temperament may make some mothers anxious and insecure about their parenting.

Mothers who are not confident may blame themselves for the child being difficult, and these feelings of anxiety will then be transmitted to the infant, compounding the problem.

Australian researchers are looking into this area of children needing help because their particular temperament clashes with a parenting or teaching style.

In paediatrics today doctors are taking a new assessment approach where the whole relationship between parent and child is taken into account and whether or not there has been a "mismatch".

Dr Oberklaid says that in the past doctors have been able to find out about parents, but have not been very good at finding out things about the child and their individual characteristics.

"If you can't find a medical problem and no emotional problem then it is important to look at temperament. We now have the technology to do that. If, for example, we see a child with colic and we can rule out physical problems, we then look at sources of the mismatch. Knowing the temperament and profile of the infant or child helps us to understand and then counsel the parents appropriately."

DIFFICULT BABY — DESPERATE MOTHER

DR Michael Bernard, Reader in Education at Melbourne University, says when a baby or child has a difficult temperament it can lead to anger and feelings of failure in the parents, especially the mother.

CASE STUDY

TRYING A LITTLE SELF-CONTROL

LIZ says she was "blessed" with the so-called typical first and second child and their personalities were poles apart.

*Timothy was colicky . . . well, I don't know if it was colic but we certainly spent a lot of time walking him up and down the hallway to pacify him.

You would put him to bed and he would scream and scream to the stage where he was so upset he wouldn't go to sleep at all. We would take him to bed with us and that worked so it stayed that way for about three years. Then suddenly he was happy to go into his own bed and slept through the night from then on.

He went through tantrums and other kinds of difficult behavior. If you wake him from a sleep he is in a foul mood whereas if you wake Amanda she just smiles and chirps.

I'm sure I've done exactly the same things with both of them but they are so different.

I like to think I ignore Timmy's tantrums and misbehavior but every now and then my blood boils and I go 'whack'. Then I feel terrible and guilty. I like to think I am setting an example for him to control his anger so when I don't stick to my principles I feel angry with myself.*

"I can do it, I know I can."

"I believe there are three basic discernible temperaments that children show symptoms of and become more obvious as the child gets older," he says.

"They are the EASILY FRUSTRATABLE child who is very demanding — they must have what they want when they want it. They really believe they need it . . . the bike, the biscuits, the keys . . . and they can't stand not getting what they want.

"These children have difficulty following rules and patterns and often experience eating, sleeping and/or social problems. These children believe 'I always have to have what I want'. They fight with other kids, they grab things from them and they push others around. They are frequently seen as impulsive kids, some are hyperactive and some are not," says Dr Bernard.

"The second type of temperament is the SHY ANXIOUS child and the evidence suggests this is biological. About 70 per cent of anxieties are due to temperament and biology. A lot of behavior — withdrawing, shyness, non-compliant, easily frustratable — is independent of birth order and parenting style.

"The third type of temperament is perhaps the easiest for parents — NOT EASILY FRUSTRATABLE and NOT OVERLY SENSITIVE child. They tend to fight their anxieties or frustrations while the others might flee from them.

"Any two children will react differently to the same situation depending on their temperament. One will suffer discomfort in a new environment, another will be comfortable."

Dr Bernard says it helps parents to remember the child has a life of his own; he can interact with, but is not totally a function of the environment. It helps parents to cope with problems if they are aware of their baby or child's temperament, he says.

AIM FOR A GOOD MATCH

- *A good "match" between parents and child will mean harmony, a "mismatch" should be worked on.*

- *Parents need to consider the temperament of their baby or child and how they react to situations.*

- *Because no two children are the same each child will require a different response from the parent.*

- *Remember it is not the child's temperament alone which is important but the way they interact with the environment.*

- *Temperament is believed to be part biological (babies are born with personalities) and part environmental (attitudes are influenced by the environment)*

SECTION TWO

1

IT'S OK, IT'S JUST A STAGE
She'll grow out of it!

- *Stages of development.*
- *Intellectual, social, physical and emotional growth in children.*
- *Delays in development, learning disabilities.*
- *What parents can do to tap into talents and special interests.*

"**STAGES for Ages**" is not about comparing children. We have all screwed our noses in disgust as a boastful mother says, "But Johnny walked at nine months" or "Susie could read when she was two".

But parents do need to know about each stage of a baby and child's development and be prepared for any special problems each stage may bring.

Parents should remember there is a wide discrepancy between children in terms of growth and development. Not all children reach "milestones" like walking, talking or reading at the same time. However, they do need to watch their child closely and if they are concerned about things like hearing, vision, speech or understanding they should seek professional help.

The challenge for parents in child development is to help stimulate the child, to realise that "play" has a purpose. It is the baby and child's way of learning new skills. A visit to a playgroup, kindergarten or childcare centre will show the importance of a variety of materials such as sand, water, playdough and props for imaginative play. All of these are enriching activities that help develop skills and experiences.

Tapping talent or assisting a child's natural creativity is encouraged. But that's not to say every child should learn Japanese as soon as they can talk or go to the opera when they are four. They could, however, be introduced to things like music, art and theatre. How will they ever know about books if we don't show them one? And if the experts are correct in their observations — that a large part of a child's learning is in the first five years — you can't help but want to support their natural desire to learn.

It just gets back to wanting the best for our children although sometimes what we consider the best is not always what they want. As much as I would like James to learn a musical instrument he will be at footy practice long before I could get him to sit still at a piano. William? I may have a chance with the music lessons. He does like to perform.

Knowing the "stages for ages" can also help us handle the conflicts that certain ages will bring, like the bored baby stage, toddlerhood or the independent stage. It can help us see a light at the end of the tunnel.

A smoother stage generally follows a difficult one where new skills are being learnt.

Author and Associate Director of the Gesell Institute in America, Dr Louise Bates Ames, says parents often need reassurance that their child's behavior is "normal". For the informed parent, the many odd behaviors that the child exhibits as he grows do not come as a complete surprise and do not seem to be the signs that something is necessarily wrong with the child, she says.

"Overall changes in the basic kinds of behaviour occur as the child alternates between stages of equilibrium and stages of disequilibrium with maturing age," she says.

These two kinds of behavior alternate rather systematically during the ages between 18 months and 16 years, according to a number of studies.

A pattern of development that repeats itself three times between the ages of two and 16 and includes the following stages: smooth behavior, break up of behavior, balanced behavior, inwardised behavior, expansive behavior, trouble or neurotic behavior and then once again smooth behavior.

This professional view is one that many "smart" parents have already worked out — they know their child is "just going through a stage" and they recognise their role as one of helping them through it.

PLAYING WITH A PURPOSE — TAKE TIME TO PLAY

PLAYING with your baby or child is as important as feeding and bathing them. But some parents still think play is a waste of time, despite all the evidence that suggests it is essential for physical and intellectual development. During the first year a baby's play is exploratory, then it develops into manipulative and imaginative play.

Babies from their very first days are learning and they especially like voices. They like to look at things like mobiles and color. Soon they will be reaching out to touch things and hold them. The next stage is exploration when they begin to use objects and learn to bang or push. Soon after that they are moving and making sounds.

Parents can help their baby's development by giving encouragement and security. Toddlers are constantly demanding attention and assistance with their play. They like safe places to explore — a cubby house made out of a big cardboard box that can turn into a car or boat . . . a drawer or cupboard of plastic household things . . . containers to stack and fit together . . . books and pretend play. They love to get outside with water and sand. They love riding bikes and making mudpies!

Older children like to play one-to-one games with their parents — they enjoy being the sole interest of the adult. Make-believe games, matching pictures in books or reading provides quiet time together. They also desire to learn about numbers, letters and their favorite word is "why".

According to Margaret Clyde, Associate Professor, lecturer at Melbourne University's School of Early Childhood Studies, playing comes naturally to some parents while others do not try at all.

"Some mothers have to accept that having a baby or toddler and a tidy house don't always go together," she says. "Accept that some play is messy and is good for them. Play really is the way children learn about the world.

"Children who are denied quality play do suffer. It is a way for them to develop strategies by finding out about new situations. They naturally want to explore — to take things out and put them back in again. Opening and shutting the sliding door is a way of playing and learning.

"One of the major concerns I have is that parents may be exploited by toy manufacturers. Children don't need expensive hi-tech toys. Plastic containers and saucepans provide hours of fun. Instead, parents are made to feel guilty if they don't have the latest state-of-the-art toys. Things such as sand, water and other natural materials are good to play with. Imaginary games such as tea parties for older children, and imitating parents is also good fun".

Prof Clyde says parents are sometimes much better than teachers at setting up the right environment for play. Play should not be structured, which is what you want. Parents should let children go. Encourage them within limits and offer opportunities that stimulate them. Parents should also let the child play alone, she says. "Some parents make the mistake of thinking that their child's every waking hour has to be filled with interesting diversions and activities."

WHEN BEAUTIFUL BABIES BECOME MOBILE MONSTERS

MANY new parents live in fear of the "Terrible Twos" when their once "Beautiful Babies" become mobile monsters and turn orderly homes into chaos with their new found independence.

But coping will come easier to the parents who can step aside and see this new stage of development from the child's point of view. They might even find toddlerhood a rewarding time.

If the PARENT understands why it is so difficult for a two-year-old to sit still in a supermarket trolley while she shops, perhaps major battles can be avoided. Consider it from the child's perspective — to touch, smell and drop all of the wonderful attractions in a supermarket is the most natural thing in the world. To ask a child to come shopping but not to touch anything, or to stay by your side when they are surrounded by noise, color and distractions, is not natural.

Passing this testing time of tantrums and truces will generally mean a smoother, less demanding stage is just around the corner like the "Trusting Threes" or "Fabulous Fours". For many parents the mistake is not knowing what to expect and overestimating their children's capabilities in terms of behavior.

Child psychologist and senior lecturer at Melbourne

CASE STUDY

TAKE TIME TO TEACH YOUR CHILD

LYN says she knew so little about children before she decided to have one that she took to reading books to find out as much as she could.

'I really believe that most of their learning is done in the first five years and if we can find ways to stimulate them, we owe it to them. Kindergarten is too late. You have to start as early as you can but then I do know from experience that in the early days it is more a matter of survival than trying to entertain them.

I suppose the first area I looked at was language. I do talk to my toddler all the time but I make sure it is relevant. I say things like 'now we put on our jumper and show her the jumper' or 'this is the way we peel the potatoes' and show her and let her play with them. Books are great for learning and after we read the book we close it and talk about the things we remember from the book.

When we go out on a walk, which I try and make a daily ritual, my daughter will chatter about all the things she can see along the way. You have to be prepared to stop 100 times in 100 yards but it is fun and it is important. I think if parents are not aware of the stages of development they can pass you and the child by without you providing them with the challenges and learning opportunities that they need.

Of course you can fall into the trap of bringing out the wrong things at the wrong time which I have done. I have given Shelly a turn at playdough or painting only to find she is bored or not ready for it. I don't really think parents can 'push' their child too hard. They won't let you, but perhaps you need to try not to frustrate them by not providing the right stimulus or if they are very young by over-stimulating them.

I believe if a baby or child is bored and not fulfilled they will be unhappy — just like us. Some of the things I have tried with my kids are swimming, gymbaroo, books, puzzles, music and songs. We started gymbaroo when Shelley was about eight months because the equipment was good and I had read that growth and motor co-ordination come before fine co-ordination and there is some evidence that it can even help them in their intellectual development. Of course, some of the theories you have to take with a grain of salt but some make sense and if they enjoy it that's all that matters.

It helps to have new venues too. I have found the children like going to our local recreation centre, the park or friends' homes and discovering their toys. Toys are important and knowing what to choose is vital. Some people say kids today have too many but if you select the right ones they can be very useful for development. The time you choose to teach your child has to be right for both of you. If they are tired it is useless or if you are not in the right mood you are not really doing any good.

The other thing that helps is to give toddlers jobs to do. They love to think they are sharing and helping '

University School of Early Childhood Studies, Dr Jill Rodd, says parents and educators should be trying to move away from the "ages" concept as it doesn't necessarily correspond to development and all children are different. You can, however, slot children into general categories — infancy, toddlerhood, preschooler, school age and so on. Infancy is from birth to about 14 months; toddlerhood (which has early and late stages) can last up to three years of age; and the pre-school stage, from about three to five years.

Dr Rodd says the big change for infants, and their parents, is when the child starts moving, when their world be-

Mastering new skills.

comes bigger and there are more things they can do — walk, climb, explore, experiment.

"The most noticeable thing here is the increasing independence of the child," says Dr Rodd. "They now understand they can influence what goes on around them — they are assertive and often difficult to handle because they have a mind of their own.

"Many parents find here that they are lost, they have been able to deal with a baby that certainly has physical needs but is generally compliant and manageable.

"When the baby becomes a toddler parents ask 'What happened to my baby? She says no, she won't do what I ask'."

Dr Rodd says parents should be aware that there are differences between early and late toddlerhood. "From 18 months to two years they begin to really understand that they can make their parents lives easier or more difficult, that they can have an effect on what happens around them".

This is why many confused parents will be taken by surprise when bedtime or mealtimes suddenly become an issue. One frustrated mother could not understand why a child who normally ate everything declared all she would eat from now on was peanut butter sandwiches. And yet another little boy told his parents he would now go to bed when they did!

Most child psychologists agree you can forget the idea of a rational discussion or argument with a two-year-old. You are wasting your time and energy. Dr Rodd says parents should not overestimate what a young child is capable of and try not to expect too much understanding from the child.

"The key is to take the emotion out of the situation, giving a choice can sometimes help the child's frustration and quest for independence," she says. "Parents can get bound up in arguments and they regress. The skill for the parent is to decide what is appropriate behavior and what is not. Many parents find they are giving in just for peace and for some setting limits is very difficult, like deciding what time to go to bed.

"A successful technique is to ask the parent what behavior they want and what are the reasons for a particular behavior or rule."

Parents should try to understand that these periods of rapid growth are not easy for the child to live through and it may be some comfort to know the difficult times do alternate with calmer times. It is suggested these periods of "disequilibrium" usually occur during the even years as new skills are learned, and in the odd years of "equilibrium" they are perfected.

The preschooler is considered to bring a "calmer" time when at about the age of three they are starting to be co-operative and helpful. The child is very interested in learning, is curious about everything and has a creative imagination.

But the preschooler still needs to feel secure, says Dr Rodd. "Their social world is starting to expand through child care or kindergarten and they are spending some time away from the primary caregiver. Therefore their relationship with the other carers is very important, they have to trust the other person.

A three-year-old who does not feel secure can be a real pain, and not take advantage of all of the learning opportunities.

"It may be an easier period because the child now has physical competence, a good command of language and they have so many skills where they can be independent, says Dr Rodd. "They can get their own things, get something to eat, put their jumper on or off.

"The three-year-old's own needs are still important but they are less dominant and they are able to see how others feel in a situation. If a child has been hurt and needs to be comforted they will tell you or try to do it themselves, they start to have some empathy and you can say how you feel".

In the area of social development for the preschooler, it helps if the parent can now start to separate the behavior from the child. This is the stage where it is important for the child to feel good about themselves, to be competent and parents can help with praise and encouragement.

Parents should try not to be too mistake-orientated, or constantly telling the child the world is too dangerous.

"Often the physical size of the child will increase expectations as they appear to be competent because of their size," says Dr Rodd.

Children this age still require supervision and you must look at their environment to see that it is suitable. Even though they are bigger and have good language they are still not able to understand childhood accidents and dangerous situations. The challenge here is to balance the opportunities for independence with the need to protect them and keep them safe."

For the older child it is a good time to introduce "problem solving" especially in relation to things like sharing or hitting. A parent can show that there are ways of dealing with a problem other than aggression.

Dr Rodd suggests parents comment on the behavior that they like in their children. She says training in the positive things is the key, but it does take time.

Until the child is five the parents role is to help children learn, it's a teaching role and one of guidance.

"Some of the types of things we are trying to teach are:

- *what kind of behaviour we expect.*
- *how to control impulses.*
- *delay gratification.*
- *respect of other's needs and wishes.*

"We should not be on about punishment and correction and compliance with rules because they are still learning these," says Dr Rodd. "Often we get caught up in punishing children for behavior and things that they may not be able to control. That's not to say we let them do as they like that we say 'that's okay, they don't understand'. We have a responsibility to ensure others are safe and secure and sometimes have to protect one sibling from another.

So we teach that rather than hitting when we are angry we could try problem solving.

The next stage could easily be called the Fabulous Fours and Fives as with maturity comes co-operation and understanding. Parents can start to realistically expect some predicable and reliable behavior.

"The difficult things that come in here," says Dr Rodd, "are fantasy and the difference between real and unreal.

"At this stage you can start to introduce rules and they will know they have a choice about whether they break that

Remember . . . notice the good times.

rule and if they do that punishment will follow. If you have spent the last five years teaching and guiding they will have a good understanding of social convention and then you can start to talk about correction, punishment and consequences".

At this stage you've got that added joy where you can share your day with them and they understand your language.

They are forming opinions and they talk about their feelings. The child can also be swayed by reason now, says Dr Rodd.

CHOOSING PLAY GROUPS AND KINDERGARTENS

MANY early childhood educators believe children should start socialising at as early an age as possible, at least from 12 months onwards. Parents, very early on then, are faced with choices of playgroups, kindergartens, creches and child care centres. Because there classes to help them develop their self-esteem may be helpful.

But others warn that parents should not overdo it and disagree with the ideas of "hothousing" or pushing children too far too soon. The advice of many is to let children be children, let them learn to play, to entertain themselves, to just do 'normal' things and not overdo the classes and activities so that their days become so hectic there is little time for enjoyment and fun.

Gifted or talented children do, however, have special needs and attention should be given to providing the right education for a talented child. Associations for gifted and talented children exist in every state and provide support, advice and information for parents and their children.

In the same way, parents should watch out for the needs of children who show early signs of Learning Disability. This disability affects about 10 per cent of Australian children and often puzzles parents. Early detection and intervention by professionals and parents will help overcome problem areas.

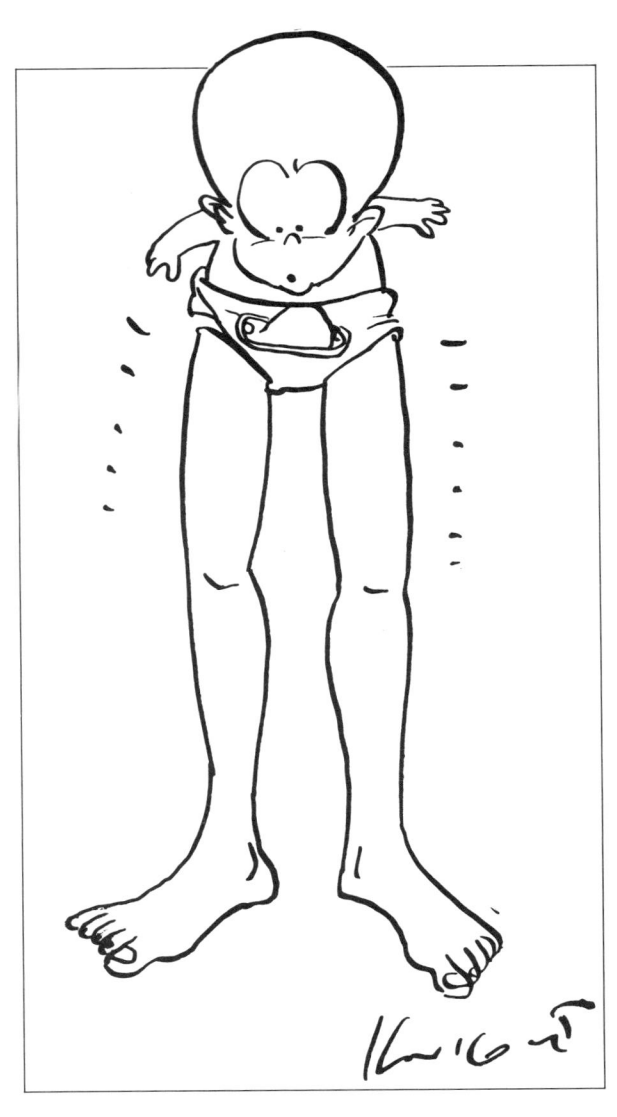

are many types of centres to choose from a good place to start is your local council which will have a list of those approved by the council as well as some of the many private operators. The local family services centres or neighborhood leisure centres are ideal for playgroups and pre-school activities.

Parents should select those ones that they are interested in and visit them. They should be thorough in their assessment. Talk to the teacher in charge and sit in on some of the sessions or classes. If possible spend some time there so you can get a feel for the routine, discipline and the environment. Have a look at the facilities and talk to other parents.

As well, there are drama groups, dance classes, music classes that are suitable for toddlers or pre-schoolers. Many parents believe that in order to help their children reach their full potential they must be stimulated and motivated. Young children, the experts agree, are receptive to learning and

STAGES FOR AGES

- *Every child develops at a different pace — try not to compare children.*

- *Read to your baby and child — he is never too young. Your voice is soothing and he will soon enjoy the pictures.*

- *Watch out for growth and development spurts — during this period your child will be learning new skills and then putting them into practice.*

- *Let your child guide you in showing readiness for activities.*

- *Talk to your child — use exaggeration and emphasis. Your child is learning the art of communication from you, the teacher.*

- *Playing is a way of learning for children and it is hard work — provide lots of stimulating play.*

- *Let your older child learn to play alone.*

- *Help your older child's vocabulary and try not to simplify — introduce new words.*

- *Seek professional advice if you are worried about their hearing, speech, vision, understanding or co-ordination.*

SECTION TWO
2

THERE'S A MONSTER IN THE HOUSE
And he's throwing a tantrum!

- Identifying types of behavior.
- Temper tantrums and blackmail.
- The purpose of behavior and getting attention.
- Some strategies and skills — letting them know what you do like.

REWARD the good behavior, ignore the bad. A pretty simple rule I picked up from the child behavioral experts on a subject that can drive parents to despair. The countless child management books I have pored over all support the theory that children play up for one reason only: they want your attention! Many parents would agree.

But trying to put rules and reasoning into action is not always easy. It is a little difficult to ignore a toddler pulling at your legs while you are talking, or pretend not to see an older son shove junior when the victim is falling on top of you. Behavior is a curious thing; why is this little boy an angel most of the time and a monster for the remainder?

If you believe what you are told — that all behavior is motivated, that the behavior (pleasing or unpleasing) is a means to an end, to have 'needs' met — then finding the right responses for inappropriate behavior is not so hard.

Stressed-out parents often overreact by yelling, hitting or "putting-down" the child which can all be harmful. I now try hard to put my responses to a particular behavior into perspective. I learnt the hard way. After a regular visit to my maternal and child health centre, I came home highly embarrassed and full of guilt. I had related to the nurse my two-year-old's constant refusal to pick up toys, and that even a little effort from the stubborn toddler would have made me happy. I explained to her that I followed to the letter a suggestion to remove the toys from him. Three days, advised the concerned nurse, may have been a fraction too long given that the young child could not even grasp the message I was giving about natural and logical consequences! Perhaps, she suggested, I tried understanding how difficult it was for a two-year-old to concentrate on something for that long. Turning it into a game of singing and sorting could have been a better solution for us.

Another strategy for the toddler tantrums that worked for me was distraction. I found it useful when two little friends didn't know how to share a toy, or when around five in the evening a toddler was so tired he couldn't think very clearly. I learned to distract, divert and dish up dinner all at the same time! With a little planning you can have your kids help wash vegetables, set the table or squeeze the juice (they love that one), but it means patience and mess.

Typical toddlerhood starts around 18 months and hits a peak around two (I have known late starters who are strong finishers) and can continue until three or four years of age. The main aim during this stage is learning methods of control and how to encourage your child to move some way towards becoming a little adult.

The controls we need to teach are that demands cannot be met immediately (but beware . . . count how many times you use 'in a minute' in one day and then try halving it).

Some of the difficulties of toddlerhood are the constant demand for attention and the parents' overuse of negatives. Children learn "No" long before they learn "Yes".

Diversion tactics.

Toddlers live only for the present and as they develop self-control they also discover that they can use a little power.

A child's second year, in my opinion, is much more complicated when it comes to behavior and understanding them. They struggle so hard to assert their independence and sometimes seem to do nothing you want. They want it and they want it NOW. Parents and educators also claim children struggle again around the age of four as they learn new skills and strive for independence which can be as frustrating for them as for their parents.

I think the path is easier if you can make it so and make it seem as if your children are making decisions for themselves. I have seen others smirk when I have asked the boys if they would like to have a bath before or after tea or if we might go shopping before or after lunch. They say I am letting the child run my life. I like to think this approach is teaching them they can make choices and learn the consequences of those choices.

Of course this is a perfect example of me, the parent, putting a theory into practice and deciding for myself if it works. I suppose it illustrates the theme "empowerment" or self-determination. Other parents say they use bribing or "behavior modification" techniques to get the desired behavior from their child, despite some critics dismissing it as outdated or ineffective. It should be is up to the parent to be flexible and comfortable in what methods they choose for themselves and their children.

We can, however, get it wrong! Shopping is one of the most difficult chores to do with a toddler or young child. During an expedition to the supermarket one of my boys decided to climb in and out of the trolley. After much pleading and discussion of consequences, I decided to follow through with the rule, "Leave, get out, go home". Well, the offender couldn't believe it — he started crying and objecting. It was one of the best tantrums I have seen with yelling and crying and kicking, but I followed it through. In the car it was a nightmare with cries of "I'll be good, I promise, I'm sorry". I somehow remained calm and repeated to the by-now hysterical child that the rule was "If you can't do what mummy asks at the shops we come home . . ." and explained that was exactly what would happen from now on. But I really wondered if it was worth it, as he was so upset and seemed to feel so bad about it.

The next time we went shopping, however, he was very co-operative and even reminded me of what happened the last time!

The fights, the tears and the tantrums aside, this period of life is also an amazing time for parent and child — a time when they are learning so much so quickly that it really does excite you. Not a day goes by that I'm not astounded by, and proud of, some little new achievement.

CASE STUDY

A DARING DAD'S 'DARLING' DAUGHTERS

ANDREW, a father of three girls aged two to seven, can't believe how differently his girls behave — there is the model child, the naughty one and the cute one.

❛We don't really believe it should be that way, but for some reason it is and now we recognise it we might be able to do something about it.

Carly who is seven, is a good child, easy to get along with, but she is very shy. Alice, who is five, is more outgoing, but cries a lot for attention and Jenny, two, plays the role of the youngest, the baby who is always cute and doing the right thing.

What I think helped my wife and I understand our children's behavior was the parenting course we did with the then Monash Parent Teacher Education Centre. I remember coming away from the first lecture feeling sick, nervous, but challenged, and saying 'this is too much responsibility'. The thing is, we didn't really have any major problems with our kids but then that's what makes it all the more worthwhile — parents don't necessarily have to do a course just because they have problems.

Too many people see it as only for those with problems and our family judged us that way too.

I believe parents are the best teachers and there isn't just one way of doing things. I think I'll still be learning when I'm 99! You can never do it perfectly all the time, but we feel we are a step closer.

Our second little girl was a constant whinger; first it was always just to get attention and then it became more of a power thing and a habit. If she did something wrong she would resort to tears. We now let her cry on her own. We say 'there are expectations in this house and one is you don't whinge to us, do it on your own'. One time our tempers would have flared and we would all end up angry and upset.

The weekly family meetings we have are good, even the two-year-old sits around the table and tries to follow what we are talking about. We have a list in the cupboard and the kids can ask us to put things on the agenda, or we put them down as they happen. Last week we lost a pet goat and the girls wanted a kitten so Alice asked her mum to make a note of it for the next meeting.

Now when the girls fight it is different; it is not for our attention but other reasons and we leave them to themselves. Recently, one child had her sister up against the wall and I told them to go into the bathroom and fight. I showed them where the Dettol and cotton wool were and I said not to annoy me unless someone was badly hurt. They forgot what they were fighting about and Carly said to Alice 'do you remember where the Dettol was?' Understanding the motives is important for us and it helps us work out our strategies.

The satisfaction of parenting comes at the times when I can sit back and listen to them and watch them playing together. I love hearing them thank each other — their openness is wonderful.

Our motto in our house is 'Have a go, Jo,' especially because Carly was never willing to try anything that she didn't think she could do.

Parents have to accept the fact that they aren't always right and learn from their mistakes. You need to have a set of principles and be consistent with them. Your kids will soon remind you of the rules anyway.

We have found we are more tolerant of our friends' children too because we understand what they are doing and why they are behaving the way they are. ❜

UNDERSTANDING IS THE KEY

PARENTS have to have a framework for understanding their children, according to Professor Maurice Balson, Associate Professor in Education at Monash University and founder and former director of Monash Parent Teacher Education Centre (now called the Monash Education Centre).

"Today so many children do not accept domination and demand equality," he says.

The task for parents is to understand the basic motivation of their behavior — the desire to belong.

Prof Balson says a naughty child is a discouraged child. The sources of discouragement range from over-protection to spoiling, rejection, competition and fault-finding. In his book, *Becoming Better Parents*, Prof Balson says to understand children and to foster their physical, intellectual, social and emotional development requires that parents have a knowledge of human behavior. This is so they can make appropriate decisions about their children and can behave in ways which are designed to stimulate their child's development.

"The desire to belong, to be accepted, to contribute, is the basic motivation behind all behavior," says Prof Balson. "It is a sense of inadequacy, a feeling that one cannot belong through constructive activity, which is at the root of all failures, deficiencies, and behavior problems," he says.

"In our society, which is so competitive and characterised by superior/inferior relationships, many children do not have a chance to feel equal with others and will pursue unsatisfactory ways of belonging, guided by the conclusion that 'I am not good enough'.

"There is nothing more important in life than a child's original family for it is there that the basis of personality is formed. Families need to develop an atmosphere which permits children to experience a sense of belonging. It is only when children feel they belong successfully to the family that they will move on in life — contributing, participating and co-operating."

Prof Balson says it is impossible to understand the behavior of any one child in a family without understanding the behavior of the other children. "Each child has chosen a way of belonging largely because of the behavior of the others; for example, Jane is responsible, George is difficult and Sally is cute," he explains.

"As all human behavior has a purpose, the key to understanding and correcting a child's behavior is to identify the purpose and then act in such a way that the behavior does not achieve its intended goal.

"It is important to recognise that emotions are created and generated to achieve a purpose. Children do not behave badly because they are emotionally upset but they become emotionally upset in order to misbehave. It is a sad commentary on child rearing that the most common method used by parents to change a child's unacceptable behavior is to resort to external pressure in the form of threats, criticism, force, punishment or deprivation. Dawdling, swearing, lying, bad habits, disobedience, teasing, bad manners, stealing and such are usually followed by punishment."

"I'll be the cute one".

The effectiveness of punishment, physical or emotional or verbal, can be judged by the frequency with which parents punish the same behavior.

Prof Balson supports this theory with the following story: "A mother recently reported that she had to intervene on a daily basis to stop the fighting between her 11 year-old son and 13 year-old daughter. She had done that since the children were young — about 35,000 times! If it is the child's purpose to gain attention, the unacceptable behaviors are perfectly logical, rational and sensible from the child's view and are, in fact, the best ways of behaving.

"To punish such behaviors is to do exactly what children want you to do and strengthens their belief that they belong when they disturb — get attention."

FINDING A PLACE TO BELONG IN THE FAMILY

ON personality, Prof Balson says each child has a unique pattern of behavior. "We all have our own particular way of behaving which distinguishes us from one another, he says. "We have a particular view of ourselves and of our relationship to the environment. This typical way of behaving may be referred to as 'personality'."

"Adlerian Psycology" or "Individual Psychology" describes personality as "style of life". Adler claims it is the guiding theme in one's life and gives unity and stability to behavior. Individual Psychology argues that to understand children we must be aware of their lifestyle; to assist in their development we must understand the factors which contribute to the formation of lifestyle.

Prof Balson says the formation of lifestyle begins at birth as infants seek to understand their world and their relationship to it. "Lifestyle is the result of a child's interpretation of his environment during the early years of life," he says. "It is not the particular experiences which the child has but rather the conclusions drawn from those experiences which determine lifestyle," he says.

"It is impossible to understand any adult without information about his first four to six years of life, which are the formative years. In this period, every person develops concepts about himself and about life which are maintained throughout life, although the person remains completely unaware of the premises he has developed for himself and upon which he acts".

Prof Balson believes early parent education is important because those first five or six years of life are critical in influencing an individual's view of self, life and others.

"Rarely have I dealt with an adolescent who does not report a series of discouraging experiences early in the home life," he says. Indeed, the test of parenting effectiveness comes in adolescence.

Individual Psychology is based on the belief that the most important factor influencing lifestyle is the child's ordinal position, the birth order within the family. Personality and character traits are expressive of movement within the family. They indicate the means by which children attempt to find their place within the family.

As Adler suggests: "Before we can judge a human being we must know the situation in which he grew up. An important moment is the position which a child occupied in his family constellation".

Prof Balson says loss of confidence is also a big factor in misbehavior:

In their efforts to find a place in the family, children meet with many difficulties.

Their initial attempts at achieving, contributing and co-operating are often discouraged by parents and children begin to lose faith in their ability to cope with the demands of the situation.

"A three-year-old boy who offers to clear the dishes from the table, help unpack the shopping, or run an errand will frequently find that his offers are refused on the grounds of 'too small', 'too heavy', 'too slow'. What the child is being told in this and similar incidents is 'As you are now you are not much good. When you are older, stronger, bigger, faster and smarter that's when you will be all right'.

Growing up can be tough

Prof Balson cites two other factors which can contribute to these feelings of inferiority. "Firstly, other children who are already more proficient in performing the various skills which are used as standards of comparison," he says. "A child is reminded that whatever he is doing has been done or is being done more proficiently by a sister or brother. 'Why don't you keep your room tidy like Sue?', 'Why don't you read clearly like Jim?'.

"A second source of discouragement is the mistaken methods of child rearing which result in the child being deprived of opportunities to experience his or her own strengths and abilities. Harmful approaches include spoiling, pampering, rejection, neglect, overprotection, indulgence, nagging, fault-finding, excessive talking, lovelessness and physical punishment."

Prof Balson says in a competitive society many parents want to be "super" parents; they want their children to have a happy childhood and give them everything.

"Children develop ideas that they belong only if they are the centre of the family and they immediately get whatever they want," he says.

"From these various sources of discouragement, children develop a sense of inferiority which impels them to strive for the 'useless' side of life. 'Useless' side of life refers to behaviors which demonstrate no interest or concern for others, which reveal a lack of co-operation, and which are directed towards personal superiority and power over others.

"If parents would set out to provide each child with a set of encouraging experiences, to refrain from criticism, to use approaches which communicate respect, to focus on a child's abilities rather than his or her disabilities, they would greatly assist children in their personal development and would lay the foundations for the development of a healthy personality."

'PROFESSIONAL' PARENTS

PSYCHOLOGIST and parent educator Carolyn Maclean has seen the results of many of today's stressed-out parents who come to the Melbourne Co-operative Family Centre seeking help. As founder and director of the centre, which has been conducting parent training groups for 15 years, Ms Maclean believes today's parents have more information and knowledge to build better relationships with their children.

"In our culture, because parents today are so continually under stress, we almost universally become aggressive and what comes out of our mouths is criticism, destructive name-calling, threats and punishment," she says. "It is usually delivered in a screaming angry voice." (Try taping yourself for a day!)

"To control children, parents are often driven to behave like terrorists and they frighten their children into submission/obedience. They do this because they are replicating the old system of reward and punishment used on them by their own parents.

Parents tend to feel attacked by the children which initiates a payback response of punishment.

The parent very frequently feels that the child knows better but is deliberately misbehaving to get at them.

"In the old system, society at large did reward unthinking obedience and workers were told what to do and how to do it," says Ms Mclean. "But we now need to prepare our children for a world in which they have to think for themselves — use initiative, be creative and be assertive — in order to win a place in the workforce.

"Because the workforce is now an unstable competitive environment our whole style of parenting has to adapt to raise thinking, co-operative, flexible, responsible children who are manifesting these qualities from a very early age."

Ms Maclean says the old system of reward and punishment parenting depended on the existence of a set of social rules that parents and children and the whole of society bought as right and proper behavior.

CASE STUDY

A TOP TANTRUM THROWER

CATHY describes her two year-old-son Tim as an adorable, lovable child, but . . . Tim was a regular tantrum thrower, at his best in the middle of big shopping centres with a guaranteed audience and plenty of room to kick and scream. With all the skill of a theatrical performer, Tim would wait and watch for the attention he craved.

❛I would just look on in despair, tears in my eyes, red in the face and my hand itching to smack! It has been hard, but as all the advice has told me, I have learned to walk away. I have learned to ignore the tantrums. It's his problem and if he chooses to carry on in front of everyone, I can't be responsible.

Of course it's not always that simple. People do look and point, and sometimes offer sympathy to me or him. One interfering old woman even picked him up to comfort him which only made matters worse.

In the past he has had me in tears, but not anymore. I suppose I found it difficult because it was such a shock to see a child behave with screaming and kicking. He was a perfect baby, very placid — that was until about 12 months of age.

He was slow getting mobile — he was a late walker which made him very frustrated. Then he had to face the competition of an older sister who was very well-behaved. I soon saw it from his view which seemed to be that the only way he could compete was to be naughty.

Now I try to work on that. I'm choosing things for Tim to do that are special for him and something his sister is not interested in or good at. He loves music and dancing so I take him to a music class for toddlers and everyone asks him about his dancing. It makes him feel good.

He still has his moments. Just recently he kept refusing to have a bath. It was his way of getting attention and it went on for a whole week. We ignored it until one night he was running around in his nappy, getting cold and feeling left out. He then decided he wanted to have a bath to get warm and join in.

I think the approach you take in discipline is only effective if both parents are supportive. It's no good changing your attitudes and not your partner's. I feel that the sibling rivalry with his older sister and my having less time with him than I did with my first child are the reasons for the big difference in temperaments in the two children. ❜

Learning to take turns.

But, she says, the reality is there are no rules.

"At the Co-operative Family Centre we take the view that each child is an apprentice; the parent is the teacher, the coach and the manager. Freud said human beings learn by being motivated through pleasure or pain. Fear, shame, deprivation and guilt do control and stamp out children's unacceptable behavior over time. But at a terrible cost to the child's self-esteem," she says. "Our centre rejoices in being able to train parents in teaching children life skills primarily through the child's own natural learning mode of pleasure.

Kids love games, challenges, races, competitions, songs, humor, poems, stories and rituals.

When these are used in teaching the child a new skill such as teeth cleaning, getting dressed quickly or putting toys away these intrinsically boring, disagreeable tasks are made interesting and important and good feelings go with the initial learning process."

Ms Maclean says the pay-off for the parents' hard work is that the child learns faster and the temper tantrums are fewer. "Mind you, you have to lower or change your expectations if you have a child who is tired, sick, hungry or over-excited or unhappy. But generally speaking a spoonful of honey does make the medicine go down!

"It only seems more efficient to employ the ordering system of 'go and clean your teeth, get into bed' and so on."

Ms Maclean says that as much as parents don't want to control their children by screaming and hitting ultimately many parents rely on that fall-back position against their own principles so the result is that many parents are in a double-bind. "Parents under stress can't invent better alternatives for the moments they need them."

"In my parent training groups we use actual replays of domestic scenes in the home that the parents can relate to — they are real life problems and then we, as a group, look at the relevant concepts and skills that would give the problem the desired outcome.

"Parents operate instinctively by blaming their children a great deal — they see a naughty, disobedient, or bad child and then they feel angry and attacked."

Parents sometimes feel helpless, betrayed, disappointed and mystified, says Ms Maclean.

"The sentences they use in their head might be something like:

- *'This child knows better . . .'*
- *'This child is just doing this to test me . . .'*
- *'I can't stand this child's behavior but I'm not sure how to handle it'.*
- *'How nasty have I got to get to make this child behave properly?'*
- *'I've done so much, I've worked so hard already, how could they now repay me by doing this to me?'*

"All of these responses are typical of an unskilled parent. A trained and skilled parent will think some of the following thoughts which are empathic responses:

- *'If I were a child of X years why would I be behaving this way?'*
- *'What basic need is this child trying to meet by this unacceptable behavior?'*
- *'If I don't like this child behaving this particular way how can I organise them into a substitute activity that will meet their needs and mine as well?'*
- *'Am I trying to get my child to surrender one of their basic needs for pleasure, stimulus, company and variety while I totally focus on my own needs?'*

"A concrete example of the skilled and unskilled parent is the often treacherous trip to the supermarket with children," Ms Maclean says. "An unskilled parent will be battling with the child and both will be hating every minute of the chore."

A skilled parent, however, will have gone through a number of steps to try and make the experience fun for all, says Ms Maclean. "They will have prepared the child for the shopping by saying things like: 'Remember, we don't buy lollies at the checkout because Saturday morning is when you get your pocket money and that's when you get to choose your surprise'.

"A good exercise for a toddler or preschooler is to have them select 12 grocery brand names from home, cut them out, put them in an envelope and take them to the shop with you. Explain to the child that it is their job to spot all the brands and match them with their labels. And at the fruit and veges area they can help count the apples or oranges."

Ms Maclean says it is important for parents to make sure that the things that kids must do are fun and interesting and pleasure becomes a part of everyday chores.

"In the old system we relied principally on logic, reasoning and morality. In this approach we put back mothering, fathering, humor and games so that everything stops becoming a battle of will.

HOW TO IMPROVE YOUR CHILD'S BEHAVIOR

- *Make chores fun with songs and games.*
- *Use action instead of words in times of discipline or conflict.*
- *Children thrive on encouragement — reward their good bahavior.*
- *Prefer the positive... look for the good and comment on it.*
- *Acknowledge the act and not the actor — in the same way discourage the undesirable behavior and not the child.*
- *The greatest influence on children is siblings — get them to co-operate and recognise each other's strengths and weaknesses.*
- *Children need to learn natural consequences — they are responsible for the outcome of their behavior*
- *Aim for consistency — children need limits and rules to follow and you should stick to them.*

HELPFUL HINTS

Give your child a card with a smiling face on it, or a special sticker, to reward good behavior... Then make sure you notice the card and praise the child. All children find the attention and approval of their parents very rewarding. Sometimes all they need is encouragement.

"Of course, your very best teacher is your own child. My daughter Anneliese at age eight said to me 'you ought to hear yourself sometimes mum'. When I began to do so, I put more thought into what I said, how I said it and why I said it. Marilyn French said 'the raising of a child is the central act to mankind'.

"I think this is the challenge we take on as parents."

SECTION TWO

3

PLEASE DON'T SMACK YOUR KIDS
Bribe 'em!

- *The importance of discipline and setting limits.*
- *Teaching positive self-talk for good self-esteem.*
- *Techniques to try and rules to remember.*

FOR many frustrated parents, disciplining children (or trying to bring harmony to the home without nagging) is one of the most difficult jobs to master and the easiest to get wrong.

Every parent knows the heartache and frustration of a supermarket checkout tantrum and subsequent battle over a Freddo Frog or lollypop, but not all parents react or cope in the same way.

To smack or not to smack . . . to give in or not to give in? Smacking, we are told, condones violence; too many "nos" foster low self-esteem; and permissive parenting results in spoilt brats.

If disciplining our children was easy, we would not feel so helpless and defeated when our four-year-old flatly refuses to go to bed, pick up his toys or constantly belts up his younger brother.

It's damned hard but it is also critical to our children's success — at school, work and in society.

While I can cope at home, it's sometimes when I'm in public, visiting friends, shopping or whatever, that discipline causes problems. Perhaps it's because I feel people are expecting certain responses from me. If one of my boys hits a smaller child, I don't want to smack him because what does that teach him? But I feel people watching expect me to — some more aggressive onlookers have even suggested I "give 'em a good whack".

How many times have we watched in horror as a mother battles with her children, smacking, yelling and bribing them? Is that the best way we have of teaching them? The classic example is the mother smacking her child because he has smacked another child. Has the child learned that violence is what you use if you are bigger, stronger and more powerful?

So much of what we do and say when we aim to discipline our children is counter-productive. The typical words we use, and the anger we express in discipline, do very little to achieve the desired outcome — good behavior. Some of the common mistakes we make include: "Because I said so", "Wait until dad gets home", "Can't you do anything right?", "Your sister doesn't do that", "Do that again and I'll smack you."

Other things we should try to avoid are threats, shouting and delayed punishment as well as smacking (some experts advise a smack could be reserved for dangerous situations like running onto roads).

Once you recognise some of the mistakes, you can work on better alternatives such as taking the anger out of discipline, which many parents unfortunately get caught up in. Better ways could be using the "soft no" in response to demands — kind, but firm.

A lack of child-rearing education and even isolation can prevent parents from sharing their difficulties with others. Understanding a range of psychological techniques is necessary in order to guide parents in their choice of child management strategies. These include problem-solving, response cost, the soft-no, controlled choices and bribing.

Having alternatives rather than one particular strategy can empower parents to choose a method that best suits their lifestyles. For example, encouragement and a reward might be useful to help a slow dresser; a fun game or ritual might improve bedtime woes; and controlled choices will come in handy in a power struggle with a child.

The trick is to remember the different techniques and to gain confidence using them at the right times.

According to some child behavioral experts, an effective method of discipline should be chosen on the basis of what kind of behavior change is desired. These include:

- *Increasing desirable behavior such as good manners and sharing.*
- *Reducing unacceptable behavior such as swearing and hitting.*
- *Teaching new behavior.*

The "response cost" approach is gaining popularity as a method of reducing undesirable behavior and increasing the behavior we do want. Basically, it means the child forgoes some privilege for misbehaving, such as losing TV time if they don't tidy their room, and then have to earn it back after "X" amount of good behavior. The idea is to have a plan or rule such as "If you hit your brother then your bike is taken away".

Another effective form of discipline can be the "time out" method. This should not, however, be over-used. The essence of time-out is not merely the separation into another room or "standing in the corner" but the removal of reinforcing (or rewarding) features in the environment. Putting him in "another room" could work if his over-riding desire at the time is to be near the adult, or doing something in the other room.

One of the best remedies I've found, however, is laughter. I can happily report it works wonders in our home. A volatile, uncomfortable or impossible situation can quickly be corrected when I break out into a silly song, pull a funny face or tell a joke. The boys giggle, I lighten up, and the pressure is off and stress levels are lowered. I also like to think they will remember how to laugh when it all gets too much.

Very few child behavioral experts consider discipline to be unnecessary and most parents not blessed with that mythical perfect child will need to use it at some stage. Besides, children do feel more secure when they have structure, when they know was is acceptable behavior and what is not. It helps parents too — to aim for consistency if they have rules that children are able to understand and follow.

While parents are better informed today than they used to be, they are also often confused by the many theories that confront them, especially in the area of discipline. The way these theories — from smacking to complete freedom — move in and out of fashion suggests that parents should choose what works for them and each of their children.

It is important for parents to also recognise that behavioral and disciplinary issues do not relate to infants. They may be appropriate from toddlerhood onwards, but even then a two-year-old is still learning. The role here is one of teaching — to show young children what is acceptable behavior and teach them ways of socialising.

The overriding messages in parenting, and in discipline particularly, should be ones of love and warmth. Without those, parents may be in deep trouble.

TEACHING YOUR CHILD SELF-DISCIPLINE

DR Marie Joyce, head of the Centre for Social Science at the Australian Catholic University, has conducted regular courses in rational parenting, including teaching children self-discipline. Parents usually attend a number of sessions and take part in practical workshops.

Dr Joyce's advice is that parents not only need help with

CASE STUDY

I YELL ALL DAY, HE'S MISERABLE

CHRISTINE'S whole world was turned upside down when she brought home a new baby and discovered her older son did not like being "dethroned".

*I thought I had prepared Josh well for the new baby and we talked about it a lot. At first he wasn't too bad because she slept most of the time. But as soon as people started noticing her, that she was rolling or sitting up, he didn't like it.

It really is a problem because he is so aggressive to her. It's not your typical sibling rivalry or a little bit of jealousy, there really is a problem with his violent behavior.

While I noticed it early on, I kept thinking he would grow out of it, that it was just a stage he was going through. I was told to ignore him, that I'm just giving him the attention he wants, but that's pretty hard when he stands on her fingers or actually kicks out at her. I find I'm continually screaming 'don't do that, don't hurt your sister' and I hate myself for it. I know he ends the day feeling pretty miserable.

I have asked him 'don't you love your sister?' and he can't even answer me. I explain to him that she's here to stay and she can be his playmate. I do try and give him special time. When I bought Megan new shoes I bought Josh some slippers so he would feel good. You sometimes wonder where you went wrong. He was my second child but after a big gap and he really was the centre of attention for many adults for three years and then along came the baby.

I really do see now that he has some behavioral problems and I have to watch his diet closely because he has incredible mood swings. Because I don't want to smack him I find I'm always yelling at him; it makes him upset and I'm sure he sometimes feels unloved because of it.

I have now reached out for help because it's not just me noticing; friends have commented on the changes in him and how he has got worse rather than better.

But I don't like it when people comment on it in front of him. He's already starting to think he is different.

When he is away with his dad or grandma he is a different kid but when it's just me and him and the baby you can see the spite on his face.

I'm starting a parenting course with a local group and if that doesn't work I'll seek professional help.*

Children love encouragement — and rewards.

Current research shows that the successful parenting style is an authorative one as opposed to authoritarian and permissive styles, which supports what Rational-Emotive theorists have been saying since the sixties (Ellis, Hauck) and beyond (Bernard, Joyce). But they've been calling it the kind and firm parenting style that promotes both disciplined behavior and self-discipline in the child.

In any discipline situation, says Dr Joyce, there are two lessons being learned by the child — the emotional and the behavioral lessons. Generally, parents are focusing on the behavioral lesson, that is, teaching the child what they expect them to do. They are less aware, however, of the emotional lesson the child is learning because the teaching here is not intentional. For example, when a parent becomes angry about a child's behavior the child learns that getting angry is the way to deal with not getting your own way.

"A lot of what's happening between people at any time, but particularly between parents and children, is emotionally charged and it's not just a matter of what you do and say but what you're feeling and what the other person is feeling while this is all happening," says Dr Joyce.

"With a discipline problem, it makes all the difference in the world if we are talking about removing a child's toys by way of punishment in a calm, firm way or doing it in a fit of rage and anger and accompanying it with verbal put-downs and abuse.

"When parents get into high levels of anger and other negative emotions they tend to get into what is sometimes called 'the emotional fog' and are able to think less clearly. When they do try to solve the practical problems they are not sensibly thought out and things are often done in the heat of the moment.

"A good technique is to calm ourselves down in the face of frustration because when a child is misbehaving or non-compliant, that's frustrating for the parent and so how the parent handles that frustration is fairly important."

Dr Joyce says people could become aware of the kind of "self-talk" they are using through Rational-Emotive Therapy (RET).

"A lot of the time parents have a conversation in their heads which is called the inner dialogue," she says. "We have habits of thought; some of that is helpful and helps us solve our problem and some of it is obstructive and only serves to build up emotions in us to a destructive level.

"We work on it in our heads; 'that little brat's done it again, if I've told him once I've told him a hundred times . . . won't he ever learn?' It builds up and feeds on our emotions, whereas if we can use calming self-talk and challenge our irrational thinking, it might be a different outcome."

Dr Joyce says teaching self-discipline is also about teaching self-acceptance.

"We teach a lot about self-acceptance for the parent and the child with a philosophy that enables the person to develop a high level of frustration tolerance and bring flexibility and problem solving attitudes to life's difficulties," she says.

"Treating them not as awful, horrible and terrible but the sort of problems one might expect to come up against as a parent.

"Thinking to oneself, 'I can't stand it when my child misbehaves this way . . .' only makes us feel worse and hinders our problem solving.

"So you might say 'my child would never do that, but here they have and it's a problem and let's see how we can deal with it . . .'

Instead of saying 'gee, this isn't too good, I don't like what's going on here', we run a horror film through our heads and turn the situation into some disaster of major proportions.

"As soon as we do that our emotions become extremely over-reactive and things can easily get out of perspective.

"Perhaps that's partly why it's easier for parents the second or third time around to know what to expect and problems are not a horror or panic situation."

Dr Joyce teaches parents how to "tune in" to their child's self-talk, to think aloud with the child and therefore provide a model for the child to think rationally about their own frustrations. So the child says to himself — 'Well, I really wanted to have that biscuit/watch TV but because I can't it's not the end of the world, just tough luck'.

"Self-talk is not so important in straight discipline, it's

more important if the child is having a tantrum or getting very upset."

"Children learn self-discipline by the external controls you place on them," says Dr Joyce. "Taking valuable or dangerous things out of reach, teaching them 'no', 'don't touch', or whatever . . . They also learn self-discipline by learning attitudes of thought. There are many irrational attitudes that we can talk about and many are more relevant when they are older but you can certainly sow the seeds when they are young."

Dr Joyce says a very important aspect of a child's development is the delay of gratification. "This comes back to frustration tolerance," she says.

"For a new baby there's no ability whatever to put off gratification. A baby can't wait for food or comfort. We can't say, 'I'll be there in five minutes', but compare that to a child of two, or even 18 months. They can wait a while, not too long, but they can wait.

"One of the important themes in teaching self-discipline is learning how to put off getting what we want right away, delaying gratification.

"Some people never learn it. So when they don't get what they want, they scream and yell. They can even become demanding, out-of-control adults.

"That process, teaching them how to delay gratification, doesn't start when they get to school. If they haven't learned any of it before they go to kinder or school they are going to be pretty difficult in the classroom. That's why parents' level of frustration tolerance is important at this early stage because they are the model for the child in how to put up with not getting what they want."

MONASH EDUCATION CENTRE A LEADER

MONASH Education Centre, which was founded by Professor Maurice Balson in the late '70s, has been an Australian leader in parent education for many years. The new director, Ms Debra Punton, says the approach to parenting today has changed out of necessity.

"We have seen a dramatic increase in inappropriate (or naughty) behavior in children and we know we have to do something to address it," she says.

"We are seeing more extreme behaviors earlier — what we used to see in adolescents we are now seeing in younger children — which leads us to reconsider what we have done in the past which is now less effective.

"Remember, children aren't born naughty they become that way. It is part of their need to belong, recognition of their place in that family. As the child becomes more discouraged, the inappropriate behavior increases."

Ms Punton says the aim of the centre, through seminars and courses, is to give parents an insight into what motivates behavior and therefore educate them to understand their children better.

"Then come the strategies and techniques to help reinforce what is appropriate behavior," she says. "We don't spend time looking for causes; what happened when they were younger and so forth. We are interested in responding now."

So how do we identify types of behavior so that we can respond with appropriate techniques? It basically falls into four categories: proposive (for gaining attention) — child misbehaves to gain attention, parents are mildly bugged by it; power (where parents are challenged) — children say "no" and are unco-operative; revenge (parents are hurt by it) — children will break parents' belongings, say they "hate" them; and withdrawal (the child feels totally inadequate, they give up) — and parents are at a loss.

It is important for parents not only to tell their child what they don't like them doing or reprimand them about behavior they don't want.

Parents must remember to spell out what the good behavior is so there are not just negatives surrounding the child.

This might mean that instead of saying "don't run in the house" we might say "the rule is we walk inside the house", or instead of saying "don't hit your brother" we might suggest "brothers are good friends. You're lucky to have a brother to play with. Why don't you have a game of cricket?".

According to Ms Punton, the goals of inappropriate behavior are tied up with how children feel about themselves; their self-esteem has a major influence on their behavior.

"The inappropriate behavior identified as power is what we are seeing more and more of," she says. "It is because kids feel more discouraged. As parents, we are constantly looking at their faults, we are a lot more protective, more ambitious and have high expectations. We are worried about the difficult world they will encounter and we want them to do well and be healthy.

"So if they are not doing well at school or not eating well, we are on to them. The child then feels, 'I can't meet their expectations' or 'my parents are constantly finding fault with me'. Parents seem to take more and more responsibility and children take less.

"When we ask parents what would they like people to say if they met their child at the age of 20, their answer is 'responsible, happy and confident'. How do we get that? It's a product of our choices. A wise decision-maker will have that confidence," says Ms Punton.

Part of the answer, she says, is freedom within limits. "Within limits, they have a choice. For example, a child of seven who goes to bed at seven o'clock has a birthday and the parent might say 'now you are eight you can go to bed at 7.10 or 7.15 pm, which will you choose?'. The child thinks 'my parents value what I think, I have a say, I'm listened to and encouraged'.

"We live in a democracy, we must give children the right to make decisions. But we are not saying let them do what they like. When a parent engages in a style that we call 'spoiling', the child grows up thinking you owe me, I can have what I like when I like.

"We cannot parent the way we were parented. The society in which we live is different, it's built on democracy, that each person is of equal value. So the past responses to punish, to smack, to reward must go. They are replaced with encouragement and natural and logical consequences."

Some examples of Ms Punton's approach are:

- *A child selects his clothes to wear for the day. It's a hot day but he has long pants, jumper and boots. He suffers the consequences (and hopefully soon strips down).*
- *A child kicks his younger brother or sister. You take his shoe off. The children want to go outside to play but you explain only those with shoes on can go outside.*

The "golden rule" with "natural and logical consequences", says Ms Punton, is that you have to make the response to inappropriate behavior reasonable, responsible and related (to the behavior).

Therefore, she explains, there is no right or wrong answer. As long as it satisfies that criteria of reasonable, responsible and related, it will feel right.

RULES WILL HELP

RULES, devised by parents and children (if the children are old enough) are the key to good discipline, according to Dr John Irvine, a child psychologist, teacher, counsellor and author. He has devised 10 easy steps for parents to discipline their children.

Parents should never try to go it alone, he says. "Research suggests parents most at risk of having problem children are not the lone parents, but the lonely ones. They should get out with other children and other adults and not be crowded in by four walls. It takes the strain off them.

CASE STUDY

A MUM WHO MAKES MISTAKES

ANNETTE says many people ask her how she copes with four children under the age of five and she tells them she "loves it but gets tired". Her biggest problems are constant fighting, meal times and misbehavior.

❛I read somewhere that the first five years are the most important and I thought, 'well, mine are all at the age, I better go and find out what I can about being a parent'. The main thing I have realised is that children always want you to give them your attention. I used to be silly enough to do it, even when they were misbehaving. But I gradually discovered that I could say 'no' and they could cope on their own. They would survive.

The first child is a dawdler and I used to do things to hurry up. Now I try to avoid nagging all the time. I have learnt to remove myself from the constant fighting which is their way of trying to get me involved. When things get bad with the fighting I try to put them outside and remove the conflict. Otherwise you get locked in a power struggle. But it can backfire.

I used to smack all the time, now I let them suffer by their own actions. By that I mean I don't get upset and angry with them. I've learnt to ignore so much more.

The children are all different. One is tidy, the other untidy. But very rarely do I have to pick up after them now because they know the rules and if they don't tidy up they don't have their toys.

I now see them copying me in the way they relate to each other but the old way of doing things still haunts me constantly. I see other parents at meal times and remember how I did it — like asking a toddler what they want. It's silly because no matter what you give them they will always want something else.

The children are always finding something to fight with you about and once I would have got angry over it, now I am more at peace and I stay out of it.

The times I slip up are early in the morning when it's too early to start thinking about natural consequences. And sometimes it all backfires, like when my youngest kept crying and I thought she was just looking for attention and I let her cry. In the end I found out she had an ear infection and I felt so guilty I had not picked it up or given her more comfort.

Shopping can be difficult when they want everything they see. We had to buy a skipping rope for the oldest girl so I said to the younger one who was shopping with me, 'We will buy one and you have to share it'. She protested and carried on about wanting two of them and I could feel people looking at me. I smacked her, realised that was wrong but it was an instant reaction and then I explained we could have one or none now and we could buy her something special next week. In the end she made her own decision and gave the skipping rope to her sister when we got home. I was proud of her.

I do look forward to 8.30 at night when the kids are in bed but I don't resent my full-time mothering. It is what I have chosen to do and for years I had my freedom. I wouldn't go back to that ever.

One big joy I get is helping them with their reading and sharing their achievements. I love it when they help you because they really want to and when they are playing and you're watching without them realising . . .

I think if every person who drives a car must have a licence then every person who becomes a parent should do a course.❜

"The big mistake parents make is to think they have to do it all, that they are less than perfect if they do not give 24-hour care," he says.

"It's okay to use occasional care to go shopping so you don't have an unhappy toddler and mum. It doesn't do one ounce of harm to leave children occasionally. If parents are afraid to leave their children, the children will feel insecure."

DR IRVINE'S 10 EASY STEPS TO DISCIPLINE

- *Determination* — to work as a team rather than pulling apart and going separately. This helps kids to find their place in the family.

- *Image* — parents give kids an image of themselves. If you expect them to behave badly they will, but if you start to expect them to behave well and show them that you do, they will.

- *Set of rules* — children must have a set of rules. They should help to develop them if they are old enough. They can't be too complicated and should be to do with jobs, privacy and ways of handling conflicts.

- *Consistency* — follow through the rules, otherwise it is no use having them.

- *Ignore the behavior you don't want.* No behavior can survive in a vacuum. This one is not always easy, but it is the most powerful.

- *Praise the behavior you want.* Children will get the message about what people like and want.

- *Learn from your mistakes.* Every parent is entitled to some. We have no training, so there is no point in feeling guilty, embarrassed or having failed.

- *Involvement* — from 18 months on, the child must be involved with other children and adults. Parents, particularly mothers, need to have their own peer group and for the kids the best discipline of the lot is from other kids.

- *Nurture their ego.* Feed their needs in terms of care, trust and understanding. Kids will be followers if their ego is being satisfied.

- *Environment* — make it work for you, rather than doing it all on your own. Use playgroups, pre-school and safety equipment. Make the environment an easier one to live in and cut down on the need to discipline.

SECTION TWO

4

MINE'S BIGGER THAN YOURS
But he started it

- *Preparing the "King of the Castle" for number two.*
- *Sibling rivalry in a competitive family.*
- *Teaching co-operation among children.*
- *Special problems of a one child or blended family.*

SHOULD you have your children close together so they have playmates and sparring partners or do you wait a few years and treat each child as an only child?

According to the experts, family "constellation" (spacing between children) and relationships with siblings are the greatest influences on a child's personality and behavior. No wonder it's such a big decision.

You would think that with seven siblings — six brothers and one sister — I should know all the answers. Mine was such a happy childhood filled with lots of love and laughter that sometimes I think eight children might not be a bad idea . . . Dad's famous line was that he was a millionaire eight times over. Mum's battle with two trolleys of food, numerous washing baskets and juggling seats in the station wagon was probably the truer story.

However, if there is one thing that stands out in all my "parenting" research it is the weight given to sibling relationships and my wholehearted agreement with the theory that a child's single greatest need is a feeling of "belonging", that they must have a place in the family.

Like my own sons, my siblings are all very different in personalities, likes and dislikes and special qualities that make them individuals. What we do share is a common set of values and we are certainly a very close family and tend to look out for one another. We share the same weird sense of humor . . . only family can get away with some thingsı

Of course there were some struggles to belong in a house that was always crowded. I remember quite vividly throwing a shoe at my older brother who had taunted and teased me to the point of no return. Unfortunately, I missed him and broke a much-loved statue of Our Lady (about a metre high and one of the few "possessions" Mum had) and I got blamed. I remember thinking 'How unfair'. Actually, I thought life wasn't fair often . . . the middle child syndrome?

With this knowledge, I now often try to think like a child when dealing with my own children.

"How did I feel when I was four and everyone seemed to be picking on me?"

My only sister and I shared a room where we had a line drawn down the middle because she was the tidy one, I was the messy one. That theme continued through the siblings — one was great at sport, the other more academic, one the clown and so on. And the only problems arose out of the competitive spirit in us all.

Perhaps my sister and I got on so well because we were not competitive, we were so different in many ways but very close. We shared lots of times and bedtime secrets and in later years we shared our sorrows.

And while the boys gave me a hard time, as I got older I liked having brothers who would take me places and of whom I was always so proud. And being in the middle, I always had younger ones to fuss over, a baby to "mother", perhaps not always to Mum's liking.

I have opted for the "close together" alternative — with only 21 months between our two boys (and another one on the way three years later). I enjoyed mothering with James so much that I was keen to have a second. All I knew was that some friends told me that sometimes having children too close together could cause more rivalry and competition than friendship and sharing.

I discovered myself, however, that the "terrible twos" might not be the best time to introduce such a major change into a toddler's life and perhaps a three year gap may have been better.

While those first 12 months were difficult, I am now delighted that the boys are so close. They do not fight and people often remark "how well they get on". I am confident it will continue because they each have different personalities. While one is competitive, he isn't when it comes to his brother. And the other is very easy to get along with as long as he feels he, too, has a special place in the family, that some things are only for him.

But I do remember how well I had to prepare the king of the household for a new arrival. Let's look at it from the child's point of view — all he knows is he now has to share his mum and dad. Here is one young child's view, on display in my doctor's waiting room:

> *Hey, God . . . about that babyı*
> *Well, Mum brought him home last week.*
> *She said I need a playmate.*
> *But, gee . . . the kid can't speak.*
>
> *He can't even kick a footy*
> *Or bowl my cricket ball.*
> *I think it was a waste of time*
> *To bring him home at all.*
>
> *My mummy used to play with me*
> *And read my favorite nursery rhyme.*
> *But now we've got that baby*
> *She hasn't got the time.*
>
> *It's 'hush, the baby's sleeping'*
> *Or 'must you make that noise?'*
> *Or 'mind you don't hurt the baby',*
> *'Don't touch the baby's toys'.*
>
> *Gran says he's simply darling,*
> *She loves his eyes of blue.*
> *I'm getting tired of all that*
> *Female "coochy coo".*
>
> *If he burps he's a clever boy.*
> *If I burp I'm just rude . . ."*

And so it goes on.

PREPARING A TODDLER FOR CHANGES

THE answer to sibling rivalry, according to the experts, is to prepare older children as much as possible and to avoid changing the family routine too much.

The child should be allowed to help in preparation for the new baby. When mum goes to hospital, he should be with someone he knows well, in his own home or where he feels safe. When the baby is brought home, ensure the household does not revolve around the baby. Encourage the child to help as much as he can. Encourage supervised play with the baby until the child can be trusted to be gentle and offer constant praise.

The arrival of a new baby in the family almost always causes some degree of jealousy in the elder brother or sister. However, jealousy is a normal reaction which is experienced by most normal children and should not be considered a problem.

With the arrival of a small, helpless human being, so demanding of time, love and affection from parents, the elder child often feels he is losing something he had before. The incessant round of lifting, pacifying, feeding and even changing the nappy might magnify his fears.

When a child has been 'King of the Castle' for a year or more — enjoying all the care and attention — they can feel displaced when a new baby arrives. Some things you could do to prepare are:

- *Encourage your child to help with preparations — the room, the clothes, the toys.*
- *Let them feel the baby kicking in your tummy.*
- *Close to the time, make sure he knows who will be looking after him and where he will be while you are in hospital.*
- *Arrange for him to visit you in hospital as often as possible.*

Looking after a new baby takes a lot of your time — an older child often has to wait for your attention and this leads to frustration for them and for you.

Be aware of the ways children might react when the new baby comes home, like demanding attention, making a fuss when people visit, occasionally hitting or hurting you, being 'heavy-handed' when touching the baby.

You can help your child by:

- *Making some special time to spend just for 'cuddles' and play — when the baby is asleep or your partner comes home.*
- *Keeping some special books or toys that you bring out for him when you are feeding the baby.*
- *Showing him photos of when he was a baby — talk about the things he did and how you cared for him.*
- *Encouraging visitors to take notice of your first child, as well as the baby.*

While at these difficult times actions speak louder than words, remember to tell your other children more than ever that you love them and that they are very 'special' to you.

Sibling rivalry is one of the most important issues in family life, according to Doctors John and Judy Kidd, co-authors of *Dr Kidd on Sibling Rivalry*.

Sibling rivalry, they claim, can turn an ordinary family outing into a nightmare and the family home into a battle ground. But it doesn't have to be that way if parents find the cause of the problems and look for strategies for dealing with them.

"Some brothers and sisters get on very well together most

CASE STUDY

NEW BABY: ATTENTION GRABBER!

RITA says she was concerned about bringing home a new baby because her three-year-old son was so used to having all the attention.

❛When Danny was three his baby sister was born. He was miserable because he felt the baby took over his top spot in the family. He was so furious that he wouldn't have anything to do with me for ages. In fact, it wasn't until his sister was two that he began to realise that she could be on his side and a real asset as a companion.

When the next baby came along, he didn't mind this baby quite as much as the first one. When he did show a certain amount of hostility I realised that if he showed a little he must be feeling a lot.

Instead of punishing him when he lost control I went out of my way to sympathise with his problems and his feelings.

Closer supervision of the baby is helpful (at least it protects the baby). But more time alone with the older child and real sympathy with the way his life is being disrupted works wonders.

I tried to do the usual things. I talked about 'his' baby. I spent as much time as possible alone with him. I planned the odd special day out while someone looked after the baby and I tried to make him feel important by 'baby-sitting' — although I have always kept them both in sight.

I especially try to help Danny see that being an older brother involves certain privileges to balance the increased responsibilities.

Sometimes he would say 'she is almost ready to play big with me, isn't she?' and I could see an increasingly good relationship and attitude developing.❜

of the time, and still inevitably have times when they get on each other's nerves," said the Kidds. "Then they scream and fight and in the process may drive the family mad.

"However, these situations are not important if the basic relationship is good. The bad times may be related to overtiredness, illness, worry, anxiety and a host of problems totally unrelated to the home or the family. They may also be due to short term problems within the household.

"In other households, children might fight continuously and unrelentingly. This can make home life like hell-on-earth with the parent or parents totally unable to control the noise, violence or the tension.

"The basic problem may be between the children or it may arise from a significant problem between the parents themselves."

What to do about fighting and competition between children? According to the authors, parents need to be referee, judge, participant and eventual winner.

"If you try for a rushed win you stack the chances against yourself," they say. "Try for winning most of the rounds and learn to wear the opponents down. Then they may throw in the towel.

"Children who have fought for years will have trouble accepting a new rule to stop fighting because they cannot see its new importance, nor can the parents define the new rule easily. It is not sensible to tell the children to 'love' each other because it ignores their innermost feelings and cannot be enforced.

"The most effective discipline is self-discipline and feuding children lack this in each other's company. However, any strengthening of their individual self-control, feeling of self-importance, or feeling of importance within the family will help strengthen self-discipline. This is a long-term approach. Children over the age of three will accept the concept of 'house rules' which are the ones everyone obeys."

On the issue of punishment in sibling rivalry, Doctors Kidd advise to be scrupulously fair. "There are few things that will perpetuate sibling rivalry as much as parents who can be conned into taking sides either to protect the supposedly hurt party or to get stuck into 'the oppressor'," they say. "Children learn very early to get their siblings into trouble."

COPING WITH COMPETITION

MOST adults can remember fighting with a brother or sister, feeling jealous of the attention the other got or feeling left out. Parents need to recognise that they can't eliminate all problems but they can help their children to co-operate and enjoy each other.

We should not compare, either. And yet I hear people doing it all the time, without thinking about the damaging effects it can have on the children.

We expect one child to be like the other and live up to things they may not be up to, whether it's school, sport or behavior.

Instead, we should be making sure they feel special because they are different.

We could also help develop self-esteem of a slower learner by focusing on their strengths or whatever it is they like to do. When they do enjoy the same things, it should be encouraged and enjoyed together by co-operation not competition.

All parents agree it is important to give some special time to each child every day. When parents are in the habit of spending special time alone with each child, it is easier for children to share parents with sisters and brothers at other times.

Even if the parents only have 10 or 15 minutes a day to be with each child, this time is valuable.

It is helpful, too, if each child can have some personal belongings of their own; a small space they can claim for themselves. Even part of a room can offer a child a measure of privacy to think and be alone when they wish.

KIDS HAVE IT ALL WORKED OUT

PROFESSOR Maurice Balson says sibling rivalry is one of the biggest areas of concern for all the parents he sees. He says children almost work out a pact between themselves:

> **"You be the clever one,
> I'll be the naughty one and you
> be the cute one."**

Prof Balson says children in each family have a different

environment because of their ordinal position. "It is not the actual birth order which is important but rather their psychological interpretation of the position," he says.

"The first born tends to be in a good position, they have a kingdom at hand, mother and father and grandparents, aunts and uncles. How unlucky they are then to be dethroned by a brother or sister. They never really overcome that: they will want to be first or best at everything. They are usually achievers, but at a price.

"The second child will be everything that the first is not. They will try to catch up to the first and the first will feel squeezed out. The last born are the nice people of the world. They are dependent and have never had any pressures. Just look at the baby books; lots of photos of the first — the first step, the first tooth, the first word — very few of the second and even fewer, or none, of the third."

Prof Balson says parents should focus on the contribution each child makes to the family by letting them help. Spacing children becomes irrelevant if there is co-operation.

"Within the family, one of the greatest mistakes made by parents is to foster competition among children," he says. "Unaware of the reasons for children choosing different ways of behaving, parents are at a loss to understand why one child is scholarly, the other unscholarly; one co-operative the other unco-operative; one noisy, one quiet . . .

"Parents lose their influence when they take sides. Their comparisons strengthen the inadequate behaviors which, from the child's point of view, are working very nicely. 'Parents pay attention to me when I'm noisy, untidy, uncooperative and do poorly at school.'

"Children influence the behavior of each other more strongly than parents do. It is important to recognise that the most important influence on a child is not a mother, not a father, but other children.

"As adult domination has diminished, the influence of the family has become more important. A family does not consist of five individuals but one group of five. Problems become 'our problems', solutions are found within the family, decisions are made by the family and 'we' and 'us' and 'ours' replace the 'me' and 'you'."

THE ONLY CHILD

AUSTRALIAN families are getting smaller, with more couples choosing to have only one child. About one third of all children have no brothers or sisters. So all the problems of sibling rivalry never occur. However, there can be problems for an only child.

Social commentators believe the Australian view of

CASE STUDY

JEALOUSY, FIGHTING, TEARS

SIBLING rivalry and jealousy have been a problem for Maryanne, mother of two, from the day she brought her second child home from hospital.

‘When the little one was old enough to become a threat and compete on equal footing it became more obvious. The older one felt threatened and we had to be aware of always being fair.

They compete all the time with school work, sport, everything they do instead of trying to co-operate. The older one may try to help out but the second won't accept it. We tell her she can only offer help but shouldn't fight about it.

The older one is a good swimmer but lately her brother has been catching up so she thinks she will give it up for fear he will soon be as good as or better than her.

When you hear them saying things like 'you're dumb, you can't even read' or 'my school is better than yours', it really grates on your nerves but I try not to over-react to such statements.

I have tried talking to my older daughter about it but she is very definite in her opinions and doesn't really listen. I think the jealousy really started with the arrival of the new baby and although I had prepared my daughter for the baby, it was not enough.

Soon after the baby arrived she developed bowel problems and she had bad stomach pains for six weeks because she wouldn't go to the toilet. We took her to a specialist and were having treatment all the time. Eventually, we got help from family counselling because it seemed that it really was a psychological problem.

She did not hit or hurt the baby. Her problem was more of a withdrawing from us. It took about 12 months before she was over it. It was hard to understand because she was a bright, articulate two and a half year old.

I can now see the whole problem as a power game and if I knew that then maybe I would have handled it differently or even better. I wouldn't have got myself so upset about her regression in toiletting.

My daughter still reacts to problems in a physical way. She bottles things up and does get physically ill over things. The younger one is different altogether and is more relaxed but he is a vengeful child.

I do try to sort out the fights and encourage co-operation but I can only do so much. It's their loss if they can't work together or help each other.’

Sport's a great energy burner.

families is both sentimental and outdated and the social consequences of smaller families which need to be addressed.

The high percentage of one-child or same-sex families means children may be ill-prepared for relationships and therefore relationships will be more volatile and likely to break up.

Studies suggest the most important thing is to improve childcare facilities. "We talk about the need for childcare for working women, but sometimes it's for the sake of our children that governments need to take action," says Prof Balson. "There is evidence to suggest that children who have that range of experiences with other children from a very early age are more socially competent and do better at school.

Prof Balson says the most serious problem the only-child faces is relating to his peers. "They live in an adult world so often surrounded by adults that they join the adult world quite early," he says. "They are precocious, more like little adults and find it difficult to get along with their peers and to be accepted.

"Their other alternative is to remain the eternal baby, to always be served by adults. Either option is not going to make it easy for them to make friends."

Prof Balson says the other major problem only-children face is the enormous pressure parents place on them. "The parents would usually be more controlled, planning people and therefore have very definite ideas for their child.

"They expect them to perform, to be successful and they are usually very bright and ambitious; they get all the attention and stimulation they need but usually in the things the parents think are important. Any child who is made to feel they have to be special is doomed to unhappiness."

Prof Balson says the consequences for the wider society are that relationships will suffer as fewer people are competent in establishing and maintaining relationships. But he adds while the problems of only-children are the most difficult for any child, the problems can be overcome.

"If parents are sensible and watch out for problems they can be overcome," he says. "The most important thing is for them to make sure the child gets in touch with other children from an early age. The playgroup network is very good and all children should be involved in it. It is very difficult for children to relate to others if they have never had the opportunity before starting school."

HOW TO STOP SIBLING RIVALRY

- *Try not to leave a new baby and pre-schooler alone together.*
- *Do try and see it from the older child's point of view — they will be feeling left out.*
- *Let the older child be the centre of attention with visitors and let them help show off baby.*
- *Talk to your older child about when he was a baby — show pictures.*
- *Give him some new privileges — on the grounds that he is older.*
- *Reward behavior you want and ignore that you don't want.*
- *Try role reversal on occasions — the younger child plays the older and vice versa.*
- *Comparing children only creates competition.*
- *Aim for sexist-free language, toys and attitudes to help foster equality among brothers and sisters.*
- *Give children time to themselves and encourage some activities separate from those with their siblings.*

SECTION TWO

5

DEVELOPING A SIXTH SENSE
The art of mind-reading

- *Learning the tricks of 'active listening'.*
- *Messages we give are not only verbal.*
- *Talking it over . . . getting kids to express their feelings.*

THIS is one question you must answer honestly. How often do you sit down and really talk with your children? How often do you really listen — without butting in or doing something else at the same time — to what they are trying to tell you?

Communication, or, the ability to express the way we feel and think with others, is essential for a sound relationship.

It must begin at the earliest age possible and requires special effort — it doesn't come naturally. It can be difficult with a baby or toddler, but every time they try to tell us something with cries, babbling and laughter we can pick up the signs and help them. This also helps improve our relationship.

Communication also raises the question of 'quality time' versus 'quantity time'. There must be time when our whole attention is focused on the child rather than just being with the child while we are preoccupied with gardening, shopping or whatever.

Much of our ability to have good communication will depend on our willingness to respect the child, to accept them as they are and treat them as equals.

It is easiest when we encourage them to express themselves, which they are usually pretty good at — like the time at the swimming pool when James wanted to know why that man had all those "pictures" on him!

If we show anger or rebuke them for expressing what they think too often, they will soon learn not to express themselves so openly. And we turn off any communication.

If we help them with their ideas, show interest and talk about the outcomes we can help them find ways to solve problems.

Asking questions like "how will you feel if . . ?" or "how will your friend or brother feel if . . ?" is a good way of getting started.

As Rudolf Dreikurs says in his book *Happy Children*, talking with our children means searching together for ideas as to what can be done to solve a problem or improve a situation.

He says when we fail to sit down with our children to talk over the current problems, we then fail to let them express their opinions and listen to them. Then they really do what they want and we lose every influence over their behavior.

At some stage in our lives, for some sooner rather than later, we will also come across the awkward, embarrassing and difficult questions children ask. We may feel uncomfortable and inadequate but we must always be open and honest in our answers.

If we have good communication and have mastered the technique of active listening (which means the parent is not silent but confirming the child's feeling and ideas and then helping them with their own problem solving), the relationship will always be free and open.

Another valued technique in the area of communication is the 'I' messages advocated by Dr Thomas Gordon in his book *Parent Effectiveness Training* and discussed later in this section.

Body language is also part of our way of communicating, particularly with young children. It's the non-verbal messages we give, the frowns, the looks we express without even thinking. I was once taken aback when my oldest son asked "Mummy, why aren't you smiling? Why have you got that look on your face"? I explained it's pretty impossible to go around smiling all day, but, yes, maybe we all could show a few more 'happy faces'.

PARENTING SKILLS PROGRAM

THELMA Paull, a psychologist and family counsellor and author of the popular *Parenting Skills Program* and *Kids Skills*, says many parents find it difficult to talk easily with young children.

"Conversations tend to be one-way. The adult tells the child what to do and there is little to no communication," she says.

"Good, clear communication is important as a background to the way parents and children get along together. It is important at the right time — after the heat of the battle, or before the battle begins!

"Children often resist conversation with parents. They resent being talked at, preached to and criticised. They often feel parents talk too much. Conversations often sound like two monologues — parent criticising and instructing and the child denying and pleading."

True communication, says Ms Paull, is based on skill and respect. She suggests some useful techniques for good communication are:

• *Be interested and try not to be judgmental.*

If you show your child that you are interested in what they think, how they feel, and that you want to hear their opinions, they will enjoy expressing their ideas and thoughts to you.

You may sometimes have to remind yourself that when you invite children to express their ideas, you have given them the right to have their own ideas, even if they don't agree with yours.

• *Encourage interaction.*

Ask children the kind of questions that will extend the conversation rather than cut it off. Dead end questions — those requiring 'yes' or 'no' answers — do not encourage interaction. You may have to ask questions that need long answers.

For example, a poor question is 'Do you have a cat at home?'. A better question might be 'What sort of pets do you have at home?'

• *Share your thoughts.*

You are your child's model for acceptable adult behavior — so you may have to think out aloud to demonstrate an adult's thinking behavior. Say when you are feeling happy, angry, sad, or if you are puzzled over something. If you practice this consistently you might find that your child will talk more about his own feelings to you. As well as sharing your thoughts, do not be afraid to be enthusiastic or spontaneous, or even admit your errors to your child.

• *Understand the feelings you hear.*

At times a child's words do not tell the whole story, and

Illustration by Chris Fisher

he may not even know his own feelings. Messages given should preserve the child's and parent's self-respect. A good method is to make a statement of understanding first.

For example, you might say 'you seem very worried about . . .' or 'you sound very disappointed . . .'

If your understanding is right, you may be able to talk about what to do. If you are wrong, you have given your child a chance to tell you what is really worrying him.

- *Be an active listener.*

Usually when we listen to people talking, we only listen partially because we are trying to put together our own piece of the conversation — when the speaker stops for breath, we hop in to say our piece!

Active listening involves hearing what your child says, putting that message into your own words and saying it back to him. No criticising, no advising, no lecturing, no smoothing over, no demanding — just listening and then giving back the message in your own words.

Ms Paull says parents need to avoid the use of active listening when either you or your child is angry about something or when your child is trying to gain your attention inappropriately.

The next step, according to Ms Paull, is to give clear messages to your children. Often it is the parent who needs to have feelings acknowledged and considered.

"The children may be annoying you, they may be interfering with what you are doing, or you may become locked in conflict with them over something," she says.

"At these times it is important to give clear messages to the children concerning the way you are feeling and thinking. You then give the children a chance to know what is going on inside you AND you give them a chance to work out a way to be helpful.

"Practise giving clear messages but don't feel guilty when they don't work. Sometimes you will need to give orders to your children, and at other times it will be impossible for you to stay cool and calm and reasonable."

Ms Paull says that when things go wrong, be constructive not destructive — deal only with the event by pointing out what has to be done and don't make negative remarks about the child's personality such as 'you're so clumsy'.

When things do go right, give the child a realistic picture of his accomplishment. Don't make comments about his personality like 'you're such a good boy'.

This view of praising or encouraging the efforts and contributions of children is reiterated often by child psychologists and family therapists and is one worth remembering.

We should look for those good things so that instead of the day being filled with nagging and yelling, it is filled with compliments and smiles for things like trying hard to make the bed clean up the room set the table.

How often do we stop and say to our children when they are playing well together, "I really like the way you are playing with each other, it looks like you're having a lot of fun"? Try it, it's a good feeling getting a smile full of surprise (and pride) from them.

ABOUT SEX AND SEXUALITY

PARENTS are often embarrassed, confused or feel awkward when their children ask questions about sex and sexuality. Many do not have good memories of their own education which was usually filled with myths and inaccuracies.

But while they want to provide more complete information for their children, they sometimes don't know how to tackle it. There are a number of organisations that run programs for parents, and children starting from a very young age.

The Family Planning Association has a simple brochure full of good advice and organises programs for parents. The Social Biology Resource Centre also provides continuing education through direct consultancy, education and training programs and research and information services.

Ms Judith Jones, educational consultant with the SBRC,

says developing children's attitudes and values about their body is essential in any sex education.

She says parents should talk about their own attitudes and values and explain them.

"Good positive sex education in the home is about direct open communication that includes values as well as information, the preferences and views of the parents," Ms Jones says.

"It is very legitimate for parents to feel awkward and unprepared. Many have had no useful experience in openly discussing sexuality issues.

"There was a heavier taboo in previous generations, but not discussing sex and sexuality can lead to a false association for some children."

Ms Jones says colloquial expressions like "playing with oneself" or "playing doctors and nurses" were shorthand for what was fairly common behavior for children.

Ms Jones says it is only natural for a parent to be concerned or anxious about masturbation, given the values that exist in our society. However, they should remember that it is very common; something like 90 per cent of all people have experimented with some form of self sexual exploration, and it is normal.

"If it is not acceptable to the parents," she says, "they should let their children know and give them some appropriate guidelines."

So, instead of responding with a smack or telling the child not to do it, they might explain their own views to the child and let them talk about their feelings.

Anne Jungwirth, also a consultant at the SBRC, advises parents and child care workers on talking to children about sex and sexuality.

She says most children are intensely curious about sexuality and are fascinated by their bodies. Knowing about their bodies and what they can do is part of their normal learning and development. They want to know how they compare to others. Are they normal? What are the differences between girls and boys, men and women? And what about babies? Where do they come from? How did they get there? How did they get out? If children aren't given satisfactory

CASE STUDY

WE TALK ABOUT EVERYTHING

LORETTA says she was always concerned with expressing her feelings to her children and encouraged them to share their own feelings with her.

❝I never smacked them. I always talked to them. During a temper tantrum when they were younger I would have just held them tight and waited until they settled. Later I would have told them how embarassed I was and how they had not behaved well.

We have always communicated well and I love to listen to them. Sometimes that listening to each and every one of them has been very draining but it means I have an open and honest relationship with each child and they can come to me and talk about anything. It's exhausting but it's more exhausting if I had to worry about them not talking to me and then running into problems.

They have six very different personalities. The first is shy, academic and responsible; the second is powerful, independent. She toilet trained herself and walked early. The third is slower, a real plodder but gets by . . .

It has meant I have to treat each of them as individuals and deal with them differently. Different situations have different effects on them. For example, the more sensitive one would react to something more seriously than the one who is more down to earth.

Getting them all to bed at night would sometimes take two hours and usually involved breastfeeding the youngest, bottlefeeding the next, reading a story to the next and then talking and reading to the others until each one was tucked in. I would sit down for a few minutes and then it would all start over again. One would have a nightmare, one would be sick, one wanted to go to the toilet and so on . . . I don't know how I survived. I suppose I was running on nervous energy.

But for me, there were many rewards that just seemed to increase with the number of children. Their smiles for one thing. They are very affectionate with me and with each other. They never suppress their emotions and I encourage them to let it out. Just the simple things in those early days were precious like their first words, the endless cuddles and kisses, their first day at school, their first school report.

And they change so much so quickly. The greatest change I noticed was from prep to first grade. They really became their own person then, although from my point of view I think the umbilical cord has never been broken

I am a great believer that everyone is born with a special gift and I have enjoyed finding that in each of my children. Whether it's being athletic, academic, or having a nice way about them, I have tried to develop their special qualities.

You never stop worrying about them — every minute of the day. It's more emotional pain than physical exhaustion now because it hurts to see them worried or upset about something, from exams to sport and relationships.❞

Special time with Dad.

explanations, they will certainly come up with their own, she says.

Children's peak in language development occurs between the ages of two and five years, a time when they are making sense of the world from the centre of their own universe, their body. They have labels for hair, nose, ears, legs and arms; it is important they have labels for their genitals.

Ms Jungwirth makes an important point that children are more susceptible to abuse if they do not have language or ability to communicate about their body parts. By labelling something "down there" or "your privates" a child is less likely to understand this aspect of their body or to feel a sense of control over it. While it is okay for families to have pet names for these parts, it is important that the child also knows the correct term, such as penis, vagina and anus.

"Not to be overlooked is the importance of demonstrations of affection, love and acceptance within the family," she says. "The non-verbal messages that you communicate through hugs, smiles and other displays of affection are all important learnings about sexuality."

Ms Jungwirth stresses that parents shouldn't feel paranoid about giving perfect answers or try to cover all the technicalities. However, open and honest communication with your children about sex can assist them develop healthy attitudes and responsible behaviors. Taking the cue from your child when they ask about such things as condoms, babies and tampons, is an important step. Providing opportunities to discuss sexuality is another.

Ms Jungwirth says that parents should accept that sexuality is an important aspect of life. It is something that should be talked about in families and not just as a subject of jokes or innuendo.

PERSONAL SAFETY

PARENTS must also see it as their responsibility and duty to educate their young children about things like "stranger danger" and "personal safety". One aspect of the personal safety program that is now taught in many schools but can start earlier in the home is aimed at prevention of child sexual abuse.

The focus of the program is to teach children about their rights.

> **Children have the right to feel safe and be safe. They can talk about anything with people they trust.**

When dealing with children, parents might talk about non specific problems and use techniques for problem solving like: "If Mary was being touched in ways she found uncomfortable or confusing, what could she do to feel safe again?"

COMMUNICATION AND LEARNING DISABILITIES

GOOD communication can help with learning disabilities, in particular reading. In the book *Reading Rescue*, Dr Michael Bernard and co-author Susan Gillet place great emphasis on communication.

"There is little question that good communication is essential for a successful parent-child relationship," they say.

"Communcication is the basic way in which both you and your child share feelings and ideas, arrive at mutual understanding of each other, and resolve the inevitable hassles and conflicts which exist in any relationship. The way you communicate with your child has tremendous impact on him as a person, on how you resolve conflicts, and ultimately, upon the relationship between the two of you.

"The messages you send your child are so important because they often say something about him as a person and, therefore, directly influence your child's self-concept and feelings of self-worth.

"The language you use with your child provides the climate for your child's growth. If the messages you send your child are heavy with evaluation, moralising, criticism, blame and condemnation, then your child will feel unaccepted and begin to distrust you and turn off.

"We strongly believe that verbal and non-verbal messages your child receives should demonstrate as much as possible your inner feelings of acceptance of your child.

"Basically, communication consists of two ingredients; sending information about how you think and feel; and receiving information from your child about what he or she is thinking, feeling, and wanting. We often make mistakes of communication with our child which lead to increased conflicts, lowered self-esteem to an overall unsatisfactory relationship.

"An essential ingredient in good communication is the capacity to listen to your child when your child seems to be upset about something or has a problem. We cannot over emphasise how important listening is in promoting our inner feelings of accpetance and trust in your child.

"Many parents are too quick to give their opinion, advice, logic, and to analyse their child who appears unsettled about something or someone. When your child communicates to you, it is frequently because he has a feeling about something. Your child may be crying because another child took a toy away, or is sad because he or she has no one to play with, worried about making friends, or frustrated with homework.

"Effective and active listening involves trying to understand what your child's message means, what he is feeling before offering your own ideas.

"A second important communication skill is required when your child's actions interfere with your enjoyment of life and create unpleasantness around the house for both you and other members of the family."

Thomas Gordon, founder of Parent Effectiveness Training, has identified different types of messages that parents may send when they are having hassles, which often leads to some very undesirable effects on their child.

They are:

ORDERING, DIRECTING, COMMANDING

"Stop making so much noise."
"Why don't you go out and play?"
"Clean up your room now."

WARNING, ADMONISHING, THREATENING

"If you don't stop that, you are going to get it."
"Father is going to get angry if you don't let him read the paper in peace."

EXHORTING, PREACHING, MORALISING

"You should always clean up after yourself."
"You must never take something without asking."
"You ought not to waste time when you have to be ready for school."

JUDGING, CRITICISING, BLAMING

"You should know better."
"You are a bad boy/girl."
"You are a very thoughtless child."

NAME CALLING, RIDICULING, SHAMING

"You're a spoiled little child."
"Do you like making me ashamed of you?"
"You're a lazy, ungrateful child."

"All these messages, if repeated often enough, will wear away whatever good you try to accomplish with your child," says *Reading Rescue*. "A key to confronting your child effectively when you have a hassle is to tell your child how you feel about his or her unacceptable behavior," say the authors.

The previously discussed ineffective messages all begin with the word 'you'. These 'you-messages' which serve to make your child feel inadequate, resentful and hopeless, have a negative impact because they appear to your child as an evaluation of him.

The book suggests you send 'I-messages' rather than 'you-messages'.

The 'I-messages' are understood as facts by your child because they communicate how you honestly feel about your child's behavior but they do not say something about him. For example, 'I get extremely worried when you are not home on time' or 'I am angry because I have asked you to play quietly so I can enjoy the news'.

"You will be pleasantly surprised at the change in your child's attitude towards you when you start to use 'I-messages'," says the book. "Parents who begin to use 'I-messages' report that children seem to listen more and respect their parents' wishes."

HOW TO BE A GOOD FRIEND

- *Be interested and try not to be judgmental.*
- *Encourage interaction — taking turns to talk and listen.*
- *Parents should share their thoughts and feelings with their children.*
- *Start communicating while your child is young.*
- *End each day by reminding your child of something he did well during the day.*
- *Active listening is an important way of showing your child that you are interested in his point of view and will help him solve his own problems.*
- *Be prepared for some things you won't like hearing.*
- *On difficult subjects find out how much the child wants to know — don't go into great detail if they just want a simple answer.*
- *Be approachable and honest in your answers.*
- *If you are embarrassed say so, but still try to let them know your opinions.*
- *Parents should convey their own attitudes and feelings, especially for older children on more contentious issues like homosexuality, AIDS, or drugs.*

SECTION THREE

1

WHEN GOD CREATED MOTHERS
He made them soft . . . and strong

- *Heartache of motherhood — to return to paid work or not.*
- *Choices women face — raising the status of motherhood.*
- *Post-natal depression and burnout.*

MOTHERS are unpaid nurses, teachers, psychologists, cooks, cleaners and handymen and, in more than 50 per cent of cases, contribute to the family income with "paid" work.

Yet many women still battle with feelings of guilt for leaving babies or children while they go out and work and unhappiness if they are full-time mothers and don't want to be. Of course there are some who seem to have the perfect balance — a lifestyle that suits their children, their family and themselves.

I have been lucky enough over the past few years to enjoy an ideal balance between family and work — ideal because it has suited our family. There have been long stretches of full-time motherhood where I did not work outside the home, but they have been interspersed with periods when I did enjoy some part-time work.

In many ways, the issue of working women divides us and instead of being judgmental about choices of careers and childcare we should be supportive. As one mother commented: "I hate the way women lie about how they are coping. The more honest and open we can be, the more support we can offer each other."

Mothers, in general, share that feeling of society's unsupportive attitude towards them. They do not get the respect and recognition they deserve.

In Finland the government pays parents about $1000 a month to stay at home and care for their children up to the age of three. That values their work at about $250 a week which, considering they work a 24-hour shift, seven days a week amounts to around $1.50 an hour. Still, it is better than nothing which is exactly what Australian parents get for their contribution.

The Women's Action Alliance, a group supporting the view that women at home should be paid an allowance, is demanding that the traditional domestic stereotype be re-examined and wants recognition for the valuable contribution of women in the home.

It is calling on the Federal Government to pay financial recognition to domestic work including a childcare payment to all women. The alliance also wants a second tax-free threshold to be applied in the household income — supported by many as income-splitting.

But it seems many mothers feel guilty, unhappy or exhausted whichever path they follow — working outside the home or not. Those who prefer, or must for whatever reasons — economic, career or sheer sanity — perform paid work have their fair share of concerns. They often feel guilty for leaving their children, guilty for wanting to get away from their children, or guilty for enjoying what they do.

Some mothers who have chosen to stay at home to be with their children may suffer too — often in silence and isolation.

They try to justify their decisions to themselves or other people. They may be quite convinced that being a full-time mother is best for their children but they may, in fact, hate it.

Some women in this situation feel they have nothing to talk about when it comes to socialising with other adults. Some mothers, fathers and grandparents can feel scared to talk too much about their children for fear of sounding "boring" when in fact it can open up discussion on a whole range of subjects such as relationships or spiritual needs (questions of identity, why are we all here?).

But in particular, it helps them get in touch with their own childhood experiences. Because we all have so many mental blocks about our childhood, talking about it with others and seeing things in another way may help us all in parenting and relationships. Kids are a good way of getting back the art of conversation.

Another important consideration, for new mothers in particular is the experience of "loss". Parent educator Constance Jenkin, who runs regular parenting groups for new mothers, says some women say the birth of their first child is a bit like being hit around the head with a baseball bat. It really is a crisis point in their life and can make women very unnerved, she says.

Ask any new mother about her losses and at first she can't think of any as she has this lovely, new baby, says Ms Jenkin. "But after a while, the responses start flowing. They include loss of sleep, freedom, spontaniety, relationship, job and recognition (there is no wage at the end of a week's work)."

Even parents armed with all the fore-knowledge of babies and parenting can still be thrown out when the baby arrives. What is important, however, is to look after yourself. Every day you need to do something for yourself, even if it's only having a cup of tea without any interruptions — instead of while you're folding nappies or rinsing bottles.

Illustration by Chris Fisher

"So, what do you do all day?" It has a familiar ring for those mums who are at home doing a job that is often under-valued. Here is a quick rundown on a "typical" mother's busy day:

6.06am: *Wake to the sound of crying baby. Baby not serious, doze off.*

6.09am: *Wake to the sound of crying baby. Baby is serious, get baby, feed in bed.*

6.32am: *Toddler awake, greets you with a lovely smile and good morning kiss and the smell of last night's dinner.*

6.36am: *Change first two nappies of the dozen for the day.*

7.15am: *Breakfast. Husband leaves for work. Toddler wants to feed himself and baby. You grab some toast and coffee. Toddler spills drink. Call to older child to get dressed.*

8.21am: *School child wants sports clothes, toddler jammed the cat's tail in the door.*

8.42am: *Baby cooing, toddler playing, mum doing dishes and phone rings. Time to get to school.*

8.59am: *Baby screaming, feed in carpark. Do 40 pelvic floor exercises. Toddler rubs vegemite toast into car seat.*

10.06am: *Feed baby, bath baby, toddler hops in. Both put to bed. Mum cleans kitchen, hoses down highchair, waxes legs and drinks half a cup of decaf.*

11.20am: *Baby crying, wakes toddler. Feed baby, change nappy, dress toddler handing him some fruit. Pack the car for playgroup. Discuss bedwetting tips and techniques and Princess Di's failing marriage.*

1.12pm: *Unpack the car, start lunch; no margarine, settle for dry, dry biscuits and fruit. Phone rings.*

2.39pm: *Baby asleep, third load of washing on line. Toddler playing in sandpit. Mum pulling out weeds, toddler helps and yanks out petunias as well.*

3.22pm: *Pick up older child from school with forms filled out for excursions and coins counted into envelopes for raffle tickets.*

4.00pm: *Sanity saver Play School is on TV with two intrigued children watching and rocking a well-fed baby.*

4.30pm: *Supposed to peel veges, kids make pancakes, scrape flour off walls.*

5.30pm: *Dinner is served but children declare they no longer like spinach pie. Encourage, assist, play games and resort to bribery for peace of mind about their failing nutrition.*

6.00pm: *Dad and unexpected visitors arrive home for tea. Zap a microwave dinner, bath kids and try to be pleasant.*

7.30 pm: *Bedtime round one. Story, kiss, hug, drink.*

7.38 pm: *Bedtime round two. Another story, then they tell you one and another lovely big hug.*

10.10 pm: *Unexpected visitors leave. Time for your bath but no hot water left. Baby awake, hungry or just overtired? Husband wants to talk about your day!*

CASE STUDY

ROBIN IS BETTER OFF WORKING

ROBIN has always combined work or study with mothering and feels her whole family is better off for it.

'I think I have been much happier with outside interests and the children learn to adjust to change easily. I started back at work when my first son was about six months old. It was great for both of us; it gave me intellectual stimulation and got me out of the house and it gave Joel a chance to mix with other kids his own age, something he didn't have much of when I was at home.

I suppose I was fortunate because I was able to breastfeed and where I worked there was a creche facility so I could visit him during my lunchbreak to feed him. It used to be hard leaving him when he got a bit older. Sometimes he would say he would really cry and I would feel miserable all day. I nearly gave up the whole idea. One day, though, I forgot something and ran back to creche and within a few seconds I could see he had settled and was playing happily. When my second son was born he started there too and they both enjoyed it.

It was hard combining work, a bit of study, the children and running a home but my husband was great. He would take over with the kids and sometimes on the weekend he would disappear with the kids all day. Grandparents were good and very helpful and the whole extended family has helped make life easier, especially if I was facing exams or was particularly busy at work.

I felt happy and confident in the care they were getting. Now we are in business together and the children understand the demands of work. We talk to them about it and we make sure we are there when they need us.

I have really enjoyed parenting. I wanted the kids very much and I don't think women have to give up what they enjoy or try to be supermum. I have kept time for myself and my life has really just got better and better.

The little things bring you great pleasure, like when the youngest child saved all his easter eggs up and brought them to me on Easter Sunday. And another time one of the boys left a card saying, 'I'm sorry I upset you and I'll try and co-operate'. The spelling was all wrong but it's the thought behind it that makes you think, 'well, I can't be that bad'. '

"I missed you, mummy."

IS IT ALL HEARTACHE?

THE aptly titled *The Heartache of Motherhood* by mother and author Joyce Nicholson is a frank and honest, if not depressing, view of motherhood.

"I was going to warn young women about the reality of motherhood, instead of the romanticised version on which I was reared," she writes in her introduction.

"I felt that if they knew what to expect, could plan their lives around the true situation, insist on their husbands sharing the burden, realise that motherhood would not satisfy them for the rest of their lives, then they would be able to avoid the worst of the unhappiness I experienced.

"I have come to the amazing conclusion that very few women really like being mothers. I even wonder if I liked it. Women love their children and talk about them at great length, but it is because they are their main interest in, and contribution to, life, and because it is still a stigma for a woman not to have children.

"If children are being discussed, they will therefore have their say. They want to appear achievers in at least their own supposed domain. It has also amazed me the support I have received for my views; so many women I thought were contented mums agreeing."

Ms Nicholson says she used to tell friends the book she was writing was "about how awful it is being a mother" and one once replied: "Every night I go to bed with a weight on my shoulders and every morning I wake up and it is still there . . . I want my daughter to be happy."

Ms Nicholson says mothers carry around an enormous load of guilt. "Fate has one more blow in store for the poor mother," she writes. "She is already burdened with bearing the child and thus interrupting her career and losing her independence. Because of this she is also expected to be the child rearer and, if she chooses to work outside the home, to carry on two jobs. Added to both of these facts, and possibly worst of all, is that if anything goes wrong with the children she is blamed. A mother carries around with her an almost intolerable load of guilt."

Ms Nicholson says it is useless and wasted because there is . . . "an untold number of human beings who turn out well in spite of inadequate mothers, as well as human beings from homes in which mothers performed their roles in letter-perfect style, nevertheless, come to tragic ends".

For some, complete devotion to motherhood is not enough, according to Ms Nicholson. "The problem is that no-one prepares you for the awful side of motherhood," she writes. "No-one talks to you about the really bad things. Perhaps it is because the bad things are different for different people. I had heard enough about 'walking the floor at night'. I had a dread of dirty nappies. I had seen enough films or read books with agonising childbirth scenes. The strange thing is, that not one of these were nearly as bad as I had expected.

"No-one prepared me for the fact that I would hate doing all the things mothers are expected to do. I would hate being patient, kind and sweet. No-one told me how utterly boring it is being with children all the time. No-one described the endless, inane conversations, the constant answering of questions. Have you ever tried to answer a child's questions with merely a 'yes dear' or 'no dear'? They will not let you.

"No-one warned me how lonely it is bringing up children. They are always there but they cannot share your thoughts, your conversation, your worries.

"Finally, no-one warned me, although I now realise my mother tried, that caring for children would simply not be enough for me. It would not occupy my mind sufficiently. It would not allow me to do the things I really wanted to do. I was forever doing something I did not want to do and pushing myself to make time for what I wanted to do."

THE BLISS OF BABIES

For those throwing themselves wholeheartedly at motherhood and trying to salvage some sense from it, there are some confidence boosting and reassuring messages from English writer and mother Paula Yates in her book *The Fun Starts Here*.

Ms Yates says women have been seduced by the glossy magazine ethic of "having it all" which she says is a great lie.

CASE STUDY

LISA BELIEVES IN SPOILING

MOTHER of two, Lisa, says she is not sure she would do anything differently if she had her time again.

'My first baby never slept for more than two hours, waking up all night long. I just used to get up and walk her about, offer her food or a bottle. I was a walking zombie and I was suicidal. At one point I was walking the baby up and down the hall and I looked outside and saw the balcony and thought 'I'm going to jump off'. I felt I was going insane and my mind was ready to snap. I woke my husband crying and crying.

I felt I was a good mother, that I was always there for them and did everything I could but I needed my own space; my space was always being invaded by them even in the middle of the night.

I did look for help but I was afraid to give my daughter any sedatives and I tried homeopathic treatment instead, but even that worried me so I just persevered.

Perhaps I should have sought professional help. The only help to me was the other mothers from the playgroup who supported me and said they felt the same way.

But the feeling you have of going insane or of suicide is so real it doesn't really help. With the benefit of hindsight, I would say I did suffer from post-natal depression and I should have sought help, but the doctor I went to didn't seem to think anything was wrong with me.

I was totally devoted to my children. I didn't work and don't think mothers should. We had a few social outings and I went to yoga one hour a week, but that wasn't enough. I needed my husband to take over just for a while, but his idea was that the mother should be with the kids 24 hours a day. He would organise outings with family and friends. All I wanted was to be on my own, to have some privacy.

I think that went on for about four years. I had no family as we lived interstate. They were the hardest years of my life and I don't know how I survived them. I don't miss babyhood at all. I did enjoy some things but mostly I didn't enjoy it. When they got older and more independent is when I started to enjoy them.

Perhaps I did too much for them but I don't know if I would do it any differently if I had my time again. I had done a lot of psychology and looked at the area of emotional release and I felt I was doing the right thing by attending to their every need. I did not want them to grow up traumatised by anything I had done or not done. My husband used to think I was spoiling them but my heart would tear if I left them to cry.

I think it had benefits. My kids today are independent and trusting and responsible, which I believe I was able to instil in them early on in our relationship. I've seen a friend's child who has been left with grandma since she was young and I know she feels unwanted and unloved. She tells her mum that she (her mum) doesn't care. She seems to have very difficult emotional and behavioral problems because of being left so much.

Young children need to feel they are the most important people in your world. We all like to feel special.

I think the advice for mothers going through what I did is to seek help, to sing out and tell someone and say 'I need help', whether its physical or emotional. It should really be someone you know very well that you can talk to honestly or someone you are happy to leave your baby with if you need to see a doctor. '

"You cannot be a biological mother only," she claims. "The very word embodies all those things we believe to be essential: nurturing, care, teaching, kindness. To deprive a baby of these is to stunt her growth, both physically and mentally."

Ms Yates goes on to say some members of society now view babies as an "optional extra to be picked up during quality time like the family dog". Her messages is loud and clear: "If you are indifferent to children, don't have them. Babies NEED their mothers."

IS IT JUST STRESS, BURNOUT OR POST-NATAL DEPRESSION?

AUTHOR of *The New Mother Syndrome* and mother Carol Dix says post-natal depression can afflict any new mother and is one of the last taboo subjects in today's society.

"Perhaps as we progress through the '90s all that will change and we will not only be allowed to talk about it but maybe even find some cures," she says.

"While 80 per cent of all mothers suffer from a brief spell of baby blues immediately following the birth, post-natal depression is more long-term and debilitating."

She adds that hormones and metabolism can cause PND as well as some underlying cultural causes such as the widely promulgated myth that birth and motherhood are natural and simple and require no special training.

Ms Dix says the risk of PND can be lessened if mothers follow a program before and after the birth based on sleep, diet, exercise and interests outside the home environment.

"Most doctors feel that classic early blues has a basic hormonal cause," she says. "During pregnancy there is exaggerated hormonal output to hold the foetus in the uterus, to create its nest and nurture its survival. By the time a woman goes into labor, the levels of her oestrogene and progesterone, for example, are 50 times higher than before the pregnancy.

"The most acute hormonal change happens on the first day after delivery when progesterone and oestrogene levels plunge dramatically.

> **'The drop in hormones can affect us in a way similar to drug withdrawal and related symptoms. The normal adjustment a mother makes to these body changes is in fact not so much normal as heroic.**

"But many adjust less well. They might experience uncontrollable crying, no sense of reality, severe depression, lack of concern for the baby, inability to sleep, lack of appetite for food and sex," says Ms Dix.

Studies have shown that hormonal changes are irrevocably tied to major biochemical changes within the baby during pregnancy and after birth.

HOW TO GET THE MOST OUT OF MOTHERHOOD

- *Remember you are not "just a housewife": Women who stay at home are carers, teachers, cooks, cleaners and volunteer workers all in one.*

- *Neighbourhood houses offer a great range of courses or work training for women at home with childcare available.*

- *Enlist the support of family and friends — physically and emotionally.*

- *Get out for a walk or do something for yourself.*

- *Talk about the possibility of PND and what you would do about it.*

- *Summarise your lifestyle by writing a list of what you would really miss if it were to change. Fit as many of those into your new life.*

- *Avoid isolation — join a new mothers' group to share your fears and experiences of motherhood.*

- *A happy, healthy mother and wife is better than a polished floor and migraine.*

- *Use occasional childcare services that are available — that's what they are there for.*

SECTION THREE

2

MY DAD'S A GREAT GUY
But he's always busy

- *Fathers have much to offer a child's development.*
- *Changing roles of fathers.*
- *Effective fathering for busy dads.*
- *Single dads and stepdads.*

THE new man who openly kisses and cuddles his children and sings lullabies is, unfortunately, a bit of a myth. In fact, most Australian men are poor fathers. That view is shared by many children and the evidence would suggest fathers do spend very little time in positive interaction with their children, despite the advent of role-swapping (where mum goes out to work and dad stays home) and the increased number of single fathers.

The New Father, however, is emerging in the '90s in the sense that men are saying they want to improve their relationships with their children, taking them from distant to warm and intimate.

The problem, many say, is not knowing how to do it. Studies have also found that a father's absence is associated with a decline in IQ in boys, but not girls. The study went on to suggest that all children with readily available fathers fare better than those whose fathers are absent or frequently unavailable. In other words, always "too busy".

Right here I'd like to vote in my choice for "Father of the Year" and record some observations of the best fathering I have been lucky enough to see in my own husband Jon and the special relationship he has with our young sons.

While he may not do too much around the house in the way of domestic chores, we do have an understanding of our responsibilities which suits us both. It means he is happy to run the farm and help with the odd bit of cooking while the other jobs are mine. For me and the boys, the important thing is that everything he does he does with them.

And, fortunately, he felt comfortable from the time they were as big as his hand (he has a huge hand); maybe that's why he could pat them off to sleep better than me.

From the time they could follow him out to the shed or paddock, he has involved them in his work. Now he has to stop building or digging long enough to play a game of cricket or get the bikes out. It is obvious to our sons and to anyone else that he loves doing it.

Jon seems to revel in fatherhood. He shares the parenting wholeheartedly and enjoys his time alone with his sons. He is good at it too. He is fun but he is also firm and kind. He has not read one parenting book but seems to have a natural "feel" for the right approach.

I think Jon, and the growing number of fathers like him, enjoy their fathering because they have variety — family, work, sport and hobbies. This is exactly what women want too - a balance.

The boys are learning from their dad all the time and Jon takes great delight in letting them tackle new and difficult things. Unlike me, he will let them try to climb the ladder or hammer nails and if they fall or fail it doesn't really matter. I would rather not watch that challenging character-building stuff.

James and William turn to their dad as often as they turn to me. He is not only a provider but a nurturer as well. They go to him for cuddles and kisses as often as they come to me. Sometimes it hurts just a little bit when I think they see dad as more fun than me because they seem to do more interesting things. But that's a good thing because it makes me work harder at keeping up with him.

I have heard both mothers and fathers experience this conflict over attention from their children in the same way kids compete for love from parents. I think it can only be good for everyone if it reinforces the importance of the family.

DADS 'DON'T HAVE TIME'

ACCORDING to recent studies, men still do not spend enough time with their children. In the Australian Institute of Family Studies report, *Children in Australian Families*, more than half of the 402 children surveyed said their fathers worked too much to spend time with them and 32 per cent said they were simply too busy.

Director of the institute, Dr Don Edgar, says many children long for more time with their fathers. "Children miss having a father who communicates," he says. "They wish he would stop working and start listening and caring. They suffer lower self-esteem because this powerful figure seems to see them as unimportant.

"The fact that almost half the adult potential for child development is being denied to children is not just a shame, it is a national disgrace."

Dr Edgar says men can no longer pretend they don't have time for children when women manage to find it as well as working outside the home.

"Such a male cop-out must be exposed and the importance of male input to parenting reasserted," he says. "One might assume from the way most men handle parenthood that they are there simply to sire offspring, bring the money in, come home, as the children in the study say, sleep.

"When we asked them (children in the survey) what dads did most of the time, we got a lot of 'sleep', not to mention 'watching television', 'sitting around' and the traditional 'gardening', 'fixing things' and ' yelling and drinking'.

The message from the experts is loud and clear — men

should become more involved if their children are to reach their full potential.

This potential is not being used because fathers do not realise their importance and society still has its mind set on the ideology that children are a woman's responsibility.

Dr Edgar says until that view can be turned around, children and fathers will keep missing out. He adds there are obvious class differences in the way men relate to their children. The father's education level seems linked to whether he talks and plays with them.

"We have found that the fathers who are the worst are those who have their own businesses or are entrepreneurs," he says. "They are preoccupied with making money and have traditional views of their role. We found the more flexible the father's work and the more they dealt with people, the better they related to their children.

"Skilled workers related well in that they could transfer their skills to kids and show them things they did around the house. The better educated professional was usually more aware of his role with his children," says Dr Edgar.

The question here, though, is even if the educated and informed father is aware of his role with his children and of the importance of his spending quality time with them, is he actively pursuing that ideal? Does he then make an effort to balance his work and family life to incorporate both?

Dr Edgar says the answer for the negligent father is simple: "It doesn't mean they have to go out and quit their jobs - they just have to take an interest in what their kids are doing. They should talk to them, read to them, go for a walk with them or look over their homework without interfering."

Men have resources, intellectual capacity and skills, just like women have, but most of these are not being put into child rearing.

It is the kids then who miss out — and the women. As one mother suggests: "Women cannot get on to an equal plane until they can be confident that the men are taking full responsibility for the childcare. Women get tired of being asked questions about the baby or child when they feel the father should be doing his own research and discovering."

Dads need to try their own things with their children and share in discussion of techniques and tactics which becomes essential for dealing with problems the family faces as the child develops.

Paul Amato, in his report The Growth of Competence which is part of the Institute's Children in Australian Families study, says: "Fathers have been found to be as competent as mothers in meeting the basic caregiving needs of infants, such as getting babies to drink a given amount of milk while bottle feeding. Similarly, fathers have been found to be just as responsive as mothers to infant signals such as crying and smiling."

And an international study has found that up to one third of babies are more attached to their fathers than mothers. Active fathering can be closely linked to high-achieving children, according to research carried out here and overseas.

A recent study conducted in America found that

CASE STUDY

OLDER MAN, BETTER DAD?

PHILLIP has trouble admitting he was a lousy father to his three children from his first marriage. He says he is now making up for it the second time around.

❛When I first became a father in the early '70s I was probably working 60 hours a week in my job. I didn't take any time off when the babies were born, I wasn't even with my wife during labor.

It's hard to say it now, but I know there was never any opportunity for bonding with the kids. I didn't change a nappy and I even felt uncomfortable holding them when they were very young.

My wife never really challenged me about it. For us, that was just the way it was. We had pretty clearly defined roles of what were her responsibilities and what were mine.

I like to think I made up for it as the kids got older like when it was time to take them places — to sport on Saturdays or special school functions. I made an effort to be at the important events but there were times I know I let the kids down and the trips away for work were never easy on them.

With this extra bonus of fatherhood a second time I am doing it differently. I now work only 40 hours a week and there are days when I rush home early to be with the kids when they are not too tired or hungry to play.

I think I bore a lot of colleagues at work with all my talk of the kids. I let them know when they took their first step, spoke their first word and all the funny things that they say and do. They really give me great pleasure and more rewards than my work has ever done.

The whole family is better off for my involvement and sharing the workload with my wife means she is happy in motherhood and still enjoys her profession. ❜

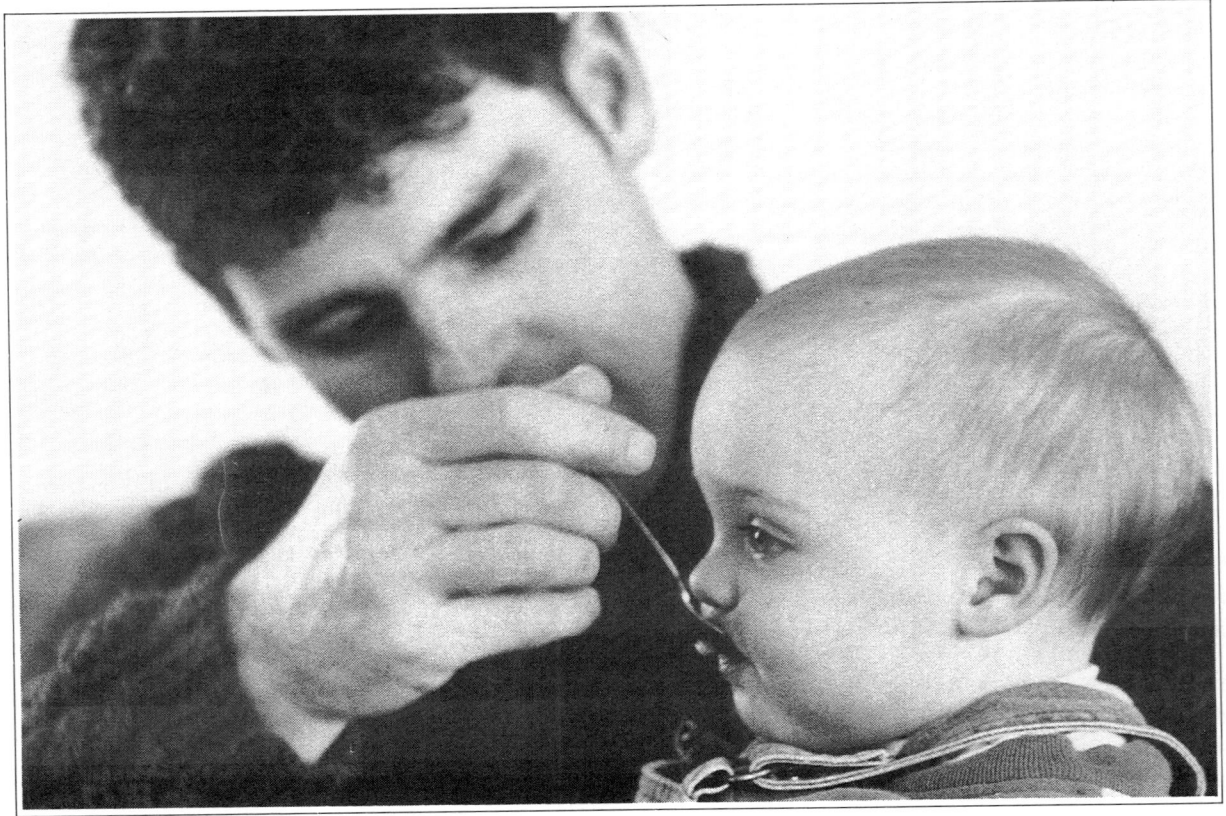

It's Dad's work too.

father involvement actually fostered more successful sons and daughters. The Emory University study says the involvement is most valuable when fathers offer support in the non-traditional areas of development.

The study tracked 248 middle-class men who had children for the first time in their mid 20s. The team tracked child care involvement, work progress and the children's educational and career success by the time they had reached their mid 50s.

The findings suggested: high achieving girls had fathers who supported things like athletic training and were emotionally close to their daughters during their teen years — teaching them to drive and taking them to karate lessons and on camping trips.

> **One study found that high achieving boys had very nurturing fathers in the first 10 years of life.**

These fathers were directly involved with their children — cuddling and rocking them to sleep as infants or comforting them when they were afraid of the dark. But the fathers had pulled back more emotionally during teen years.

The research evidence suggests that, whatever the involvement, fathers influence their children's development directly and indirectly through interaction and by virtue of the impact on the family's social and emotional climate.

The Australian study found that lack of attention from fathers was linked to low self-esteem, low self-control, poor life skills and poor social competence in primary school children.

The study also found that self-esteem correlated more strongly with the child's relationship with the father than with the mother. The more the father talked to the child, the higher the level of self-esteem.

SINGLE FATHERS

ACCORDING to recent research on single fathering, many traditional stereotypes about the roles of men in relation to home and family have not changed as significantly as some would suggest.

A study of single fathers revealed that some areas were still very difficult for them, such as the attitudes in the community, the courts, the schools, real estate agents and practical things like changing rooms in swimming centres. It found that until more fundamental problems such as equal access to work and issues to do with gender were addressed, the New Man would remain a bit of a myth.

Fortunately changes are occuring. These changes include things like the chance for men to participate in the social aspects of pregnancy and birth, find nurturing jobs, debate

CASE STUDY

DAVID AND SINGLE FATHERING

ANYONE can do it if they want to, says David on single fathering. "I guess I might be different to the stereotype, but I don't believe its impossible for males to do what I've done.

'The qualities and the capabilities are there. A male can cook, clean and iron as well as a female and offer the same emotional support that a woman can.

Today, at least, it is considered okay for a guy to be more involved in his family but largely men still use the excuse of having to go out and earn the money. The stereotype father of the 1920s is still very much the same as that of the 1990s."

David, father of Amy, 13, and Kerry, 11, says it was the loneliness and the boredom that got to him initially in his new role as single father.

"You can't even go to the milkbar on your own. You have to take the children wherever you go; you rely on people coming to see you. I was lucky I had a lot of support from my mum and dad and family and friends.

I was finishing a course when I was first on my own and then I went to join the workforce but I felt disadvantaged as a single parent. Ironically, my employers never really expected any of the problems of single parenting because I was a male.

I don't believe I've treated my children differently because I'm single or because I'm both mum and dad but they have had to deal with those problems of any single parent family like limited income and less energy and time for them.

Sometimes you feel really alone when it comes to making decisions about the children. Or you are the one the teachers want to see and you are the one that is there for netball and swimming and you wish you could share the load a little. As for meeting anyone else, I have no time and no interest. Maybe when the girls are older and more accepting.'

---

gender roles and show tolerance for non-traditional family forms and lifestyles."

It seems stepfathers, too, are in a special category and often feel very vulnerable or at a loss to know just what their role is in terms of care and discipline for their stepchildren, whether they live with them or apart.

One of the problems of these 'blended' families is for fathers to maintain authority with 'yours', 'mine' and 'ours' but the same principles apply to all parents — take time to be with each child, talk to them, listen to them, encourage them and enjoy all the benefits of the 'extras' like another 'father' or four sets of grandparents or 15 aunts and uncles.

Psychologist and author Jill Burrett has written an informative, easy to read book on getting the most out of stepparenting for children and parents. *To and Fro Children — A Guide to Successful Parenting after Divorce* offers ways to make the most of the past and accepting new kinds of relationships as a means of improving parenting.

FATHERS TRY HARDER

FATHER of five and director of the Brosnan Centre Youth Service, Bernie Geary, says because there are more pressures on fathers today, it is even more important they get help with their parenting.

He says the return of women to the workforce and the division of the workload in the home has meant that dad has to be more involved whether he likes it or not. The problem occurs because it goes against the tide; the changes have been so rapid and are against the traditions most men know and hang on to.

"The thing that strikes me is the difficulty dads have in breaking away from the image of their own fathers," Mr Geary says. "Very often we are our own fathers and we have difficulty in sorting out the good from the bad - what we liked and what we didn't like about our own fathers and the way we were brought up."

Mr Geary is one of an increasing number of men who are following in their wives' footsteps and joining parenting groups. He was part of a pilot program of fathers who met regularly at a local kindergarten to discuss the A to Z of being a father.

"The fathers' group was a wonderful experience and I only wish more men could share in it and benefit from it," he says. "In the middle of winter, instead of watching the footy we would sit on tiny kindergarten chairs and talk about our kids. The most times men get together are at sporting venues or in a pub and it is not always considered macho to say to a mate 'do you leave the light on for Peter when he goes to bed?'

"We used to talk about the things that were really on our minds, like what we wanted for our kids and at first the responses were the mandatory ones like good job, financial security and finally we'd say we want them to be happy whereas once we would leave that area to mum.

"Talking in graphic detail about our own childhoods, about what we liked and didn't like, was an important exercise for us, especially to do with our own fathering. Today, with all the knowledge and ideas filtering through, we have such a great opportunity to improve our parenting."

Illustration by Chris Fisher

At the Brosnan Centre Youth Service, a voluntary organisation aimed at assisting young teenagers in trouble or at risk, Mr Geary sees the results of bad parenting every day.

"A lot of our young people are parents themselves at 17 or 18 and already you can see history repeating itself and we are trying hard to break that cycle — of violence, abuse or negligence," he said.

"You have to unpick so much of the past. For too long we have just looked at the result — the broken kids — but never looked at the cause and it is bad parents.

"To say parents can't be blamed for their kids is absolute rubbish. I find it abhorrent. It's like people getting married who say, 'well, we hope it works out'.

"You can't have something as precious as kids and say, 'we hope they turn out'. There has to be a commitment. It's like the fathers who are out there washing the car like its the most precious thing in the world when the kids are made to play on their own and get so bored and start to play up because dad is always too busy for them.

"What I love to hear most from my kids is when they are talking about the things they've enjoyed most. They'll say 'wasn't it great when we went to . . .', or they laugh at the songs they used to sing in the car on holidays."

Mr Geary says fathering is easy once you let go of your images and traditions and let your natural instincts take over.

"Parenting done instinctively is just a joy," he says. "We shouldn't look at parenting as anything but what you get out of it at the time. We shouldn't be doing it for what it will mean in 20 years' time. But there is enough of parenting left to chance and there's already a sense of lottery about it so the better-equipped parents can be the easier it is."

HOW DADS CAN ENJOY THEIR KIDS

• *Body contact and hands-on involvement from birth is important like letting baby lie on your chest.*

• *Fathers can be just as nurturing as mothers for young babies and attachment should begin back then.*

• *Try to spend some special time with each child — a walk with a toddler, listening to a preschooler's day and helping an older child with homework.*

• *Talk to your children about your work or your day and when you are doing things around the house.*

• *Let children help you — it may take longer but they grow up so quickly.*

• *Studies have shown that children who have a lot of time with their fathers are more confident and emotionally secure and higher achievers.*

SECTION THREE

3

WHEN COUPLES BECOME PARENTS

Bridging the gap between work and family

- *Children as contraceptives!*
- *The changing face of families — blended, one-parent.*
- *Having fun as a family.*

WHEN I look back at those early months of parenthood and actually count the times my husband and I had alone as a couple, it comes to the grand total of zero.

There was a family wedding, but James was there too, adding his voice to the choir. There may have been the odd restaurant attempt but they usually failed miserably unless there was a kind waiter willing to amuse a bored baby.

The first time we got out minus baby, cot and half the house in tow, was for another family wedding which was great fun but not exactly "alone".

It wasn't really a problem, though, because as new parents we were infatuated with every move of the baby for a long time. But I believe everyone should devote time to their relationships and as one mother said: "I sometimes wish we could be how we used to be, and do the things we used to do".

Perhaps the hardest thing for a couple to face is their changing roles. For mothers, in particular, life changes dramatically; for men not so much. At times, some women may resent that.

New mothers, however, need to consider the "changed" relationship in a positive way. As one mother commented: "I don't want things as they 'were' — we have grown so much with our new baby and this is a chance for a whole different relationship. Sure it's more complex, more intense and more work but for both of us it is also more rewarding".

Some of the women I interviewed were concerned about their lack of interest in sex after childbirth and in the early years of motherhood. Perhaps it is true that children really are the best form of contraception.

Some new mothers, though, said they felt guilty and angry about confusing thoughts on sexuality. They were happy to find comfort in numbers, in knowing others shared their worry, but were still at a loss of what to do about it.

They said they had fallen into the "mother-not-a-lover" syndrome and didn't know how to break out of it. Usually they were too tired, too scared and too preoccupied with the new baby to think of sex.

But for many couples there is sex after childbirth! They cited a fuller, richer kind of sex that matured a man as a husband and father, and a woman as a wife and mother.

For some couples, however, post-natal depression can become a very real problem. Support and professional help should be sought. Latest research from the UK suggests that dads also can suffer from depression and may be in need of help!

Couples do need time alone to rekindle the fire . . . to actually talk to each other without interruptions. Not only do they need the occasional romantic dinner or weekend away but maybe they need time together every day, when the children are asleep or busy playing.

Families also need to take time to be a "family", to have fun together and to "create happy childhood memories" that will not only improve relationships but help children in their own parenting one day.

In this way the unit can become a "nurturing" family as opposed to an enmeshed, or overprotective, family or splintered family where kids bring themselves up.

There seems a need to reinforce the value of family and bring back some of the "good old times" lost in our changing society. We have lost the notion of the extended family and neighborhood support leaving many new parents battling on in urban isolation.

In the current economic climate, where many families are forced to bring in two incomes, there is the issue of shared parenting — of sharing the care of children and household jobs.

The Australian Institute of Family Studies has completed a survey on this subject and found that while more parents believe there should be a division of responsibilites in the home and care of children, much of the workload still falls back on women.

One of the emerging issues of the nineties is how people are balancing their working and family lives.

The institute's study looked at whether men are assuming more responsibility in the home and with their children as increasing numbers of women assist with the family income.

It found that while there is little difference in sex role attitudes between men and women, often their is discrepancy between what people think and what they actually do.

However, the good news is that men are contributing more in the area of sharing childcare responsibilities when both partners work.

What is clear, however, is that business and industry need to introduce more measures to ease pressure on working families — to reduce the stress for both men and women.

The workforce is still structured around the male breadwinner despite the increasing number of working women. It puts stress on couples trying to juggle home and work life and sometimes leads couples to delay having children, or decide not to have them at all.

The workplace has to catch up with the reality of family life. Workplaces need to be more flexible in allowing parents to take time off to care for sick children, in working hours, childcare assistance and family leave.

Parents need to keep in mind that they have responsibilities to their children and partners — that having fun at home with the family is just as, or more, important than contributing at work.

There are simple, inexpensive ways to putting fun back into family life and involving everyone. The local swimming centre is a perfect start — young kids just love water and you can introduce them to water safety or swimming lessons and jump into the pool with them.

> **It is a great way to achieve that physical one-to-one contact that all children crave and badly need but is often forgotten in the battle for daily survival.**

The other great family activity is bike riding — even babies should be quite safe in the specially-designed safety seats and with helmets if you ride in parks, gardens and the wide open space.

One activity that our family has particularly enjoyed is escaping to the great outdoors, getting back to nature and camping under the stars. There is not much better relaxation for the whole family than catching fish from a crystal clear stream or pounding ocean and bringing it back to the campfire where stories are stretched beyond imagination.

WHEN LOVERS BECOME PARENTS

IN her new book *The New Mother Syndrome*, English author Carol Dix, says that when couples become parents they are setting out on a totally different relationship.

Ms Dix says childbirth is an enormous life stress, especially when connected to the dreams and expectations that lead couples to wanting a baby.

Many experts tend to trivialise the strain having a child can put on a marriage.

Ms Dix says images in books and magazines also confuse us with messages that "everyone else out there is sharing baby care, having meaningful conversations in the evening, smiling benignly over the sleeping infant in the cot, and then going off to bed to have erotic, romantic sex".

A study in the United States has, in fact, discovered what most new parents have known all along — that there is a lower level of sexuality, even three months after birth. The study found that achieving orgasm after birth could be more difficult because of a number of factors — fatigue or tension, soreness after episiotomy, fears that sexual organs had changed or because of breast tenderness.

But as Ms Dix points out, more consideration must also be given to the deeper psychological strains from changing marital relationships, altered senses of identity and varia-

CASE STUDY

IS THERE SEX AFTER CHILDBIRTH?

THE thing that worried Sandra most about becoming a parent was what she saw as a deteriorating relationship with her husband.

'We never argued much as a couple but since our precious one has come along we seem to fight a lot more. It's almost natural, part of our day. Some of it is over parenting — 'you're too soft' or 'you're too hard'. And sometimes it's just from sheer exhaustion.

The thing I found very hard when I first became a mother was to think about sex. I felt that I was a mother and mothers weren't supposed to have sex. I didn't want the physical part of sex right through the pregnancy and I certainly wasn't interested after the baby was born.

Most of the time I was just physically too tired and other times I was still concerned about sensitive spots and soreness.

I think my desire to nurture my baby was more important than anything else which is the way it should be, but in that way I felt my breasts were for feeding my baby. I thought the rest of me was in such horrible shape that I couldn't bear to look at it. How could my husband be interested?

That was a very hard time for us because we had had such a good relationship as friends and lovers and all of a sudden it went downhill.

I was too tired and I thought, oh yuk, no, I'm breastfeeding . . . and then I was having sex because I felt guilty.

I was very much aware of getting upset about it all but luckily I did not fall into depression. I could understand how it might happen to some new mothers.

I felt my husband must have had problems too because he didn't really touch me, he felt my breasts were now my baby's and not his, or mine for that matter! But that was totally in his mind.

He was having his own problems dealing with this great attachment I had to the baby and wondering where he fitted in.

I suppose we were both able to overcome our problems with a lot of hard work, especially my taking time out to respond more appropriately to his needs, but there was a lot of heartache and searching as well.

I worked harder at our relationship and realised it was important to the baby that we all complement each other. **'**

ble moods: "Such is the pressure on us to be having healthy (that is, continuous and frequent) sex lives that we dare not own up to abstinence," she says. "Where once we might have been ashamed to mention having sex, now we are ashamed to mention not having sex!"

But this is changing in the nineties when men and women both seek equality and need support with their changing roles. Unfortunately many books still talk about sex as something women can do without and something men can't do without!

With the push for people to take control of their own lives the pressure should be off both men and women.

CHANGING SHAPES

THE traditional nuclear family is disappearing and in its place we have single parent families, blended families of natural children and step children, as well as a growing number of defacto relationships and childless couples.

According to the Australian Bureau of Statistics (1989) the traditional family of working father, stay-at-home mother and dependents accounted for only 16.6 per cent, or less than one fifth, of all families.

And the trend is towards more divorce, delayed marriages and delayed childbearing. But while the notion of what a family is might have changed, there is still a feeling that the family is the single most important thing for many people.

FAMILIES HAVING FUN

CONSTANCE Jenkin, a leading parent educator who has conducted courses and seminars for both professionals and parents for many years, has put all her research and knowledge on parenting into a resource kit and parent handbook called *Planning Happy Families*.

Ms Jenkin says the irony of the title "happy families" is that families cannot be happy all the time, that sometimes they will be sad or angry but the goal is to be happy more often than not.

"One of the essential things for a happy family is for parents to recognise very early on that their children have individual personalities and values," she says.

The individuality of each child should always be taken into consideration by the parents.

"Rather than considering a baby or child as an empty vessel to be filled and managed and controlled, there should be a working relationship that continues for life where as well as the child having respect for the parent the parent has respect for the child.

"If you start thinking this way in the early stages, it happens naturally as the children grow. If a parent shows a child respect and if you show them love and care and tell them often that you love them, the relationship and respect is automatic."

Ms Jenkin agrees it is not always so simple, particularly with children who may have a personality that is more boisterous or demanding. Maybe here the parent needs to

"Let me do it, dad."

set limits for the child, but keeping in mind the respect.

"On the other hand some children who are quiet and easy to deal with may still cause worry for parents who may feel they will never have friends," she says. "Whatever their personality, always encourage them and help them in dealing with special problems they may bring.

"If we grow up believing in ourselves we won't be filled with self-doubt. Being a confident person helps children cope with stressful times."

It's often so simple but it's the simple things that we find difficult.

In line with many child behavioral experts, Ms Jenkin says she aims to teach parents to look for the positive things in their children and comment on them as a way of building up good self-esteem.

"Rather than parents always commenting on the things they don't like, they need to talk about the things they do like," she says.

"Children thrive on being told about their strengths and will continue to be challenged if they are confident. It is

Try a dose of laughter everyday.

not enough to say what not to do. Parents should also teach the right way.

"Sometimes parents get bogged down with one child in the family. They will often say 'it's his fault, he's hopeless'. For some parents doing something nice with the child is very difficult. They may need professional help or specialist help to work out why they have those negative feelings about that child. It is best to try and find something the child enjoys and do it with them, helping the parents and child rediscover each other.

"It is best to recognise that all children have individual personalities and parents need to build a positive self-image with each child and their strengths."

According to Ms Jenkin, the other major consideration in the quest for a happy family is to remember to have FUN. It seems that with the struggles between work and home many parents have forgotten about having fun with their kids.

"Families should talk to each other, be with each other and interact every day," suggests Ms Jenkin. "In this way parents are setting the foundations for their own children to become parents. We learn how to parent from our own parents. If, as children, you have not been parented in a positive way it may be difficult not to repeat the mistakes of your parents. It's what happens when we are young that helps us parent well, or makes it difficult.

"For instance, the new baby who needs to be held, rocked, spoken to, cared for learns about unconditional love and trust. But I have seen that it can be hard for those who have never been shown love, have never had anything to learn from. One family support worker who was helping a new mother care for her baby was telling her to give the baby a hug and the mother said: 'But I hugged her this morning'. She did not understand how to love unconditionally."

Ms Jenkin says parents in this situation should know that they can break the cycle by learning and getting help. It is hard work because it goes against everything they have known, but it is rewarding when that cycle of neglect is broken.

Ms Jenkin says sometimes families need to set aside time to be together by planning something they can all be involved in.

"One family took up this idea and reported great success. The parents and the three children planned all week for a special PINK meal. The children prepared pink placemats, pink serviettes, pink flowers and they all wore something pink. They helped cook beetroot, ham steak and had pink sauce on the cauliflower which was topped up with pink drinks and pink jelly . . .''

It is a good exercise for parents to stop and think about the happy memories of their own childhood and recreate them. They are often inexpensive simple activities.

I know for me — going to the pool and swimming was always fun. I can still see my mum lying in the sun (when that was allowed) or sitting in the babies' pool with the youngest of the kids while the rest of us raced off to the big pool. For our family, our neighbors and friends who joined us, it was good, cheap, healthy, fun. When I now take my boys to the local pool those wonderful memories come flooding back and there is nowhere else I'd rather be . . .

HELPFUL HINTS

One of the most important jobs we have as parents is to create happy childhood memories. They should happen naturally. Sometimes they don't, but you can plan special times like a picnic, a drive to the country or a weekend in the tent.

Ms Jenkin says these happy memories will help our children as parents: "The sad thing is sometimes you actually have to teach adults how to have fun or refresh them on ways to amuse themselves and their kids. But if you can learn how to relax when times are tough they will in fact bring down the stress.

"For many families stress is a major problem. The father often gets caught in the rat race of work and being the breadwinner and they forget or don't know how to slow down and have fun. They forget that the family is an important part of their life and requires as much work and energy as you can manage.

"And in these current times when both parents go out to work, the stress is even greater. I have great sympathy for parents who have to work and then try and find this time to have fun. It can be quite difficult and confusing for them.

"In these cases maybe they need to prioritise things and for this they need to ask themselves some questions:

- *Why did we have children?*
- *What do we want them to be like?*
- *How can we achieve it?*

Ms Jenkin says parents often share common hopes and dreams for their children and some are:

- *To be friends with them.*
- *Enjoy being together as adults.*
- *Enjoy their successes and share their lives (without being overwhelmingly involved — respect for separate lives).*
- *To be caring, loving and considerate.*
- *To be confident and have a good self-concept.*
- *To have a job they like and be financially okay.*
- *To be happy, healthy and independent.*
- *To know how to manage difficult times.*

Ms Jenkins says two important things that stand out are: that their children know how to have fun and that they are able to take responsible risks and are adventurous

She says a good exercise is to write down what you liked or disliked about your own childhood and then start to create some of those things you did like for your own children.

"In terms of the couple's relationship it is essential that it is a positive one.

"It must be a lovely home where parents show and express love. So couples need to work on their marriage and learn to negotiate and share and resolve conflict. We model that for our children and create an environment that is comfortable. Arguments do occur and it's okay as long as parents explain to the children 'we're just having really loud discussion, but we're solving a problem'.

"What most families neglect to do is sit down and talk, this encourages the children and parents to be together to talk and listen," says Ms Jenkin. "For example, in one family the idea is each person takes it in turn to talk about one good thing and one horrible thing that happend during the week so they learn to take turns, to say how they feel and to listen to each other. In many homes kids don't know what their fathers do so it's good for them to hear from dad how his week was,'' she says.

BRIDGING THE GAP BETWEEN WORK AND FAMILY

RUTH Schmidt-Neven, the Director of the Exploring Parenthood Consultancy, says bridging the gap between work and home is vital for our children's overall development and good mental health.

The Exploring Parenthood Consultancy has established workshops for senior executives of industry which look at issues like personal realationships and ways to cope with the conflicts and challenges of balancing work and home. Ms Schmidt-Neven says society must move away from the notion that these are "women's issues" and more men must be involved in the debate. "A lot of men are running industry at a very senior level. We have to educate and influence them because unless we involve men we are not going to get very far,'' she says.

HELPFUL HINTS

In many families the television can become a monster and may need some taming. Let your child choose one or two favorite programs for the day's viewing and switch the television off at other times.

"Studies have shown that the mental health of children and young people is dependent upon the presence of men and fathers as much as it is on women and mothers.

"Men exclude themselves or they don't want to get involved in areas like housework and childcare," she says. But sometimes it is women, who, on a more subtle level, exclude men from those responsibilities because they want to keep an area of control that has traditionally been theirs.

Playing together and staying together.

"Our organisation aims to establish a link between valuing the family and parenting and productivity at work. Although people may think home life and relationships have nothing to do with work, this is not the case. If there are problems at home that are unresolved then it's going to affect productivity and absenteeism.

"Companies may have invested a lot of time and money in their employees and if marital and family breakdowns occur it can have a devastating effect on work performance.

"It is in the interest of industry to do something positive. It makes economical sense too."

Ms Schmidt-Neven says the workshops conducted by the consultancy open up people's capacity to understand relationships and looks at practical applications of this understanding to everyday life.

She says industry needs to have a more humane approach to looking after its workers, and companies will be forced to make changes and become more flexible if they are to meet the changing needs of families who are part of the present and future workforce.

"Some companies take the view that building childcare facilities will resolve the problems. It's important, but it's only structural. What we are talking about is more a change of attitudes. The workshops get participants to explore their own personal issues and then take them on board at work and home."

HOW TO KEEP THE FAMILY TOGETHER

- *Turn the TV off and spend some time talking every day as family.*
- *List your priorities for using your time better.*
- *Work out practical ways to rearrange your daily schedule to include the things the family likes to do.*
- *Put more time into your relationships with other family members — forget the housework and washing the car.*
- *Get out the bikes, or walk around the park — take the kids fishing!*
- *Try swimming — it's good, cheap family fun and great for fitness.*
- *Pack the tent, or hire one, and tackle the great outdoors as a family.*

A GUIDE TO SERVICES
... where to find help

Throughout Melbourne and Australia there are services and support groups available to parents in a wide range of areas from disabilities to post-natal depression.

Often the best place to start is your local council which employs people to advise and assist you. It's their job to know the resources available to the community which means you!

Parents can get support from community service officers, social workers and the specialist and visiting staff at community health centres and family services centres in their local area.

The telephone directory, local or state, is another good starting point and the Referral and Help Page will help you find up to date listings of organisations like the the Action Group for Disabled Children through to Marriage Counselling.

A useful tip for parents is to record the numbers you may need, including medical practitioners as well as a support person or group you may need in times of stress or emergencies. It is a good idea to have after hours numbers because you just may need help when the office is closed!

The organisations, phone numbers and addresses listed are for Victoria only and were correct at the time of going to press, but the publishers take no responsibility for subsequent changes. Check your telephone directory for interstate numbers.

Australian Council for Educational Research
9 Frederick St Hawthorn 3122
Telephone: (03) 819 1400

Australian Institute of Family Studies
200 Queen St Melbourne 3001
Telephone: (03) 608 6888

Australian Institute of Rational-Emotive Therapy
PO Box 1160 Carlton 3053
Telephone: (03) 585 1881

Catholic Family Planning Centre
371 Church St Richmond 3121
Telephone: (03) 427 1233

Child Accident Prevention Centre
Royal Children's Hospital Flemington Rd Melbourne 3000
Telephone: (03) 345 5786 — (03) 345 5085

COSHG Collective of Self Help Groups
Ross House 247-252 Flinders Lane Melbourne 3000
Telephone: (03) 650 1455

Exploring Parenthood Consultancy
Telephone: (03) 830 4253

Family Planning Association of Victoria
270 Church St Richmond 3121
Telephone: (03) 429 3500

Interchange Victoria Respite Care
18 Balwyn Rd Canterbury 3126
Telephone: (03) 888 5355

Maternal and Child Health
After hours telephone service staffed by trained maternal and child health nurses.
Telephone: (03) 853 0844 — 008 134 883
6 pm to midnight Monday to Friday
12 pm to midnight weekends, public holidays

Melbourne Co-operative Family Centre
Telephone: (03) 859 2266 .

Monash Education Centre
20 Loretta Ave Wheelers Hill 3150
Telephone: (03) 562 0483

Nursing Mothers Association of Australia
PO Box 231 Nunawading 3131
Telephone: (03) 878 3304

PANDA Post and AnteNatal Depression Association of Victoria
19 Canterbury Rd Camberwell 3124
Telephone: (03) 882 5396

Parents Anonymous
Collins St Melbourne 3000
Telephone: (03) 654 4654 — 008 134 008

Parent Effectiveness Training
Telephone: (03) 742 6693

Personal Safety Crime Prevention Education Consultancy Group
Telephone: (03) 416 8600

A GUIDE TO SERVICES
... where to find help

Queen Elizabeth Centre
53 Lytton St Carlton 3053
Telephone: (03) 347 2777

Telephone Advisory Service
Weekdays 6 pm to midnight weekends and public holidays — 1 pm to midnight
Telephone: (03) 347 1793

Royal Children's Hospital
Flemington Rd Melbourne 3000
Telephone: (03) 345 5522

School of Early Childhood Studies
Early Childhood Development Unit
4 Madden Gve Kew 3101
Telephone: (03) 854 3333

Sudden Infant Death Syndrome (SIDS)
Research Foundation 1227 Malvern Rd Malvern 3144
Telephone: (03) 822 9611

Royal Women's Hospital
Women's Health Information Service Grattan St Carlton 3053
Telephone: (03) 344 2007

Social Biology Resource Centre
Bouverie St Carlton 3053
Telephone: (03) 347 8700

PARENT HELP PROGRAM
PARENT RESOURCE AREA CO-ORDINATORS

City of Footscray
PO Box 58
Footscray 3011
Telephone: (03) 688 0342

City of Knox
PO Box 219
Ferntree Gully 3156
Telephone: (03) 881 8333

Family Action
PO Box 95
Dandenong 3175
Telephone: (03) 791 5233

Alys Key Family Care
70 Altona St
West Heidelberg 3081
Telephone: (03) 458 3566

Atherton Family Centre
95 Atherton Rd
Oakleigh 3166
Telephone: (03) 568 5166

Diocesan Family Services
PO Box 576
Ballarat 3353
Telephone: (03) 053 377 150

City of Morwell
PO Box 708
Morwell 3840
Telephone: (03) 051 344 744

Rural City of Wodonga
PO Box 923
Wodonga 3690
Telephone: (03) 060 559 200

Bethany Family Support Centre
1/9 Gibb St
North Geelong 3215
Telephone: (03) 052 788 122

SUGGESTED READING

SECTION ONE

Mother & Baby **Margaret Geddes** (Viking O'Neil, Australia, 1988)

Babies **Christopher Green** (Doubleday, Australia, 1987)

Three in a Bed **Deborah Jackson** (Bloomsbury, UK, 1989)

Crying Baby, Sleepless Nights **Sandy Jones** (Viking O'Neil, Australia, 1985)

Baby Games **Elaine Martin** (Stoddart Publishing Canada, 1988)

Breastfeeding Matters **Maureen Minchin** (Alma Publications/George Allen & Unwin, Australia, 1987)

Midwives, Mothers and Breastfeeding **Wendy Nicholson** (Nursing Mothers Association of Australia, 1991)

Night-time Parenting **William Sears** (Collins Dove, Australia, 1985)

Baby Crazy **Helen Townsend** (Simon & Schuster, Australia, 1990)

The Book of Baby Massage **Peter Walker** (Bloomsbury, UK, 1988)

From Me to You **Anne Whaite & Judy Ellis** (MacLennan & Petty Pty Ltd, Australia, 1987)

Colic — Crying for Help **Carol Young** (Lothian Publishing, Australia, 1986)

SECTION TWO

Becoming a Complete Parent **James Bates** (Hampden Press, Australia, 1989)

Becoming Better Parents **Maurice Balson** (Australian Council for Educational Research, Australia)

Reading Rescue **Michael Bernard & Susan Gillet** (Australian Council For Educational Research, Australia)

Toddler Taming **Christopher Green** (Doubleday, Australia, 1984)

Coping with School **John Irvine** (Simon & Schuster, Australia, 1992)

Dr Kidd on Sibling Rivalry **John & Judy Kidd** (Transworld Publishers Australia, 1990)

Bringing Up Your Talented Child **Geoffrey Lewis** (Bay Books, Australia)

Help Your Child to Learn **Barbara Pheloung** (Tortoiseshell Press, Australia, 1986)

SECTION THREE

Children in Australian Families — The Growth of Competence **Paul Amato** (Australian Institute of Family Studies)

To and Fro Children **Jill Burrett** (Allen & Unwin, Sydney 1991)

The New Mother Syndrome **Carol Dix** (Allen & Unwin, Australia, 1985)

Planning Happy Families Constance **Jenkin** (C.A. Jenkin, Australia, 1988)

The Heartache of Motherhood **Joyce Nicholson** (Penguin, Australia)

Becoming a Father **William Sears** (Collins Dove, Australia, 1988)

Living in a Stepfamily **Ruth Webber** (Australian Council for Educational Research, Australia)

The New Explorers **Ruth Schmidt Neven** (Full Circle, Melbourne, Australian Council for Educational Research)

The author gratefully acknowledges the following authors and publishers for permission to reproduce material from these publications:

Night-time Parenting **William Sears** (Collins Dove, Melbourne, 1985)

Dr Kidd on Sibling Rivalry **John & Judy Kidd** (Transworld Publishers, Australia, Pty Ltd, 1990)

Reading Rescue **Michael Bernard & Susan Gillet** (Australian Council for Educational Research)

The New Mother Syndrome **Carol Dix** (Allen & Unwin, Sydney, 1985)

The Heartache of Motherhood **Joyce Nicholson** (Penguin, Australia)

From Me to You . . . Advice to Parents of children with special needs **Anne Whaite & Judy Ellis** (MacLennan & Petty Pty Ltd, Australia, 1987)

A Special Thank You

Thank you to Vicki Hatton for her expertise in editing and her invaluable support; Helen Gardiner for her publishing advice, encouragement and enthusiasm; Genevieve Edwards for her beautiful photographs; Mark Knight and Chris Fisher for their clever illustrations; and Ray Petrie for his innovative typesetting and design.

My special thanks also to Sally Morrell and Andrew Bolt for their creative flair and wealth of ideas and thank you to Lynda Gordon for her first-class secretarial skills.

My special thanks to my family and friends who have also contributed both directly, and indirectly, to this book which really began five years ago with the arrival of James, intensified with the "addition" of William, and became urgent with the anticipated arrival of their brother or sister!

Thank you to those who read sections, contributed ideas and helped in administration especially Margaret Wyrill, Kerry Steward, Janine Wolfe and Michele Fawcett.

Thank you also to the families who gave their time for photos including Jo and John Arnold (Jesse); Rob and Sue Langmaid (Tess); Julie Sullivan and Brian McNeill (Paris); Vicki and Paul Hatton (Aaron); Helen and Simon Gardiner (Eric); Bill and Sally Wilson (Tom, Holly and Ned); Don and Jane Grant (Imogen and Jack); Andrew and Jaci Egan (Casey and Darci); John Egan and Stacey Carter (Shea). And of course the gorgeous Jon, James and William van de Pol.

My sincere appreciation goes to my own family — The Egan Gang — who believed in the book and encouraged me all the way. Thanks to my brothers (a superhuman effort in distribution) and their families — Paul and Luke; Tom, Trina, Mathew, Michael and Nicole; Andrew, Jaci, Casey and Darci; Seamus, Donna and Derek; John, Stacey and Shea; and Matt.

And my special thanks go to those who, over the past five years, have helped me to "love being a parent" with their support — Joan and Henk van de Pol; Jo, Colin and Jack Maxwell; Helen, Simon and Eric Gardiner and Donald and Mini van de Pol.

Thank you to my extended family — especially the boy's "special" grandparents, who have loved them like their own — Margaret and Jack Simpson and "cousins" Andrew and Nick and great-grandad Les Gammon.

ACKNOWLEDGEMENTS

To the many professional people working in paediatrics, child psychologoy, parent education and family therapy who have contributed their expertise and time to this book, I am truly grateful.

Thank you to:

PROFESSOR MAURICE BALSON, Associate Professor of Education, Monash University, founder and patron of Monash Education Centre.

DR MICHAEL BERNARD, Reader in Education, Melbourne University, Director of Australian Instititute of Rational-Emotive Therapy.

PROFESSOR MARGARET CLYDE, Associate Professor, School of Early Childhood Studies, Melbourne University.

DR ROBERT DAWSON, Psychologist, Director of Australian Institute of Rational-Emotive Therapy.

DR DON EDGAR, Director of Australian Institute of Family Studies.

MS VAL FOSTER, Co-ordinator, Monash Education Centre.

MR BERNIE GEARY, Director, Brosnan Centre Youth Service.

DR CHRISTOPHER GREEN, Consultant Paediatrician, Head of Child Development Unit, Royal Alexandra Hospital for Children, Sydney.

DR JOHN IRVINE, Psychologist, READ Clinic, New South Wales.

MS CONSTANCE JENKIN, Professional and community educator, Alys Key Family Care.

DR MARIE JOYCE, Psychologist, Head of Centre for Social Science, Australian Catholic University.

MR DON KINSEY, Public Relations, Royal Children's Hospital.

MS CAROLYN MACLEAN, Psychologist, Melbourne Co-operative Family Centre.

MS PAMELA McLURE, Public Relations, Royal Women's Hospital.

PROFESSOR SAMUEL MENAHEM, Associate Clinical Professor, Royal Children's Hospital.

DR JEANETTE MILGROM, Director, Clinical Psychology, Austin Hospital.

DR FRANK OBERKLAID, Director, Department of Ambulatory Paediatrics, Royal Children's Hospital.

PROFESSOR GILL PARMENTER, Pyschologist, Head of School of Early Childhood Studies, Melbourne University.

MS THELMA PAULL, Psychologist, Family Action Dandenong Valley.

MS DEBRA PUNTON, Director, Monash Education Centre.

DR JILL RODD, Psychologist, School of Early Childhood Studies, Melbourne University.

MS RUTH SCHMIDT-NEVEN, Psychotherapist, Royal Children's Hospital; Director Exploring Parenthood Consultancy.

DR AMANDA WALKER, Department of Paediatrics, Monash Medical Centre.